Praise for
Upsizing the Indivi ̄
in the Downsized Orga

"For all the words written about the new sl
is one book that finally matters. It doesn't p
are here yet, but it does give a meaningful ~~~~~~~~~ ~~~~~~~ ~~~~~~ ~~
th   d,
b

"The authors kee~~~~~~ li-
zation and propose an alternative vision. ~~~ ~~~~~~~~ ~~~~~ or a net on
a dock. Pick up a node of it and you get a temporary hierarchy, pick
up another node and the hierarchy remolds itself. Put the net down
and the hierarchy disappears. The authors seem to grasp—as many
companies do not—that it takes a lot of skilled fishermen to handle
nets."
—*The New York Times*

"This book is a must-read for individuals living with reengineered, re-
invented, restructured, and redesigned organizations. It is an exquisite
exposition in how they can cope, prosper, and enjoy their new lives."
—William H. Davidow, author of *The Virtual Corporation*

"Astute, sensitive, timely, and readable. This book is about working effectively in the 'fishnet organization'—a useful metaphor."
—*Future Survey*

"[Johansen and Swigart] examine the problems that have arisen because of downsizing, such as increased uncertainty about individual
roles, the loss of 'corporate memory' and continuity, and declining operational loyalty. . . . This thoughtful book should appeal to managers
and general readers alike."
—*Library Journal*

"A book that can help people find fresh ways and new opportunities
to thrive in the emerging organizational environments."
—*Booklist*

Upsizing *the* Individual *in the* Downsized Organization

Managing in the Wake of Reengineering, Globalization, and Overwhelming Technological Change

Robert Johansen *and* **Rob Swigart**

ADDISON-WESLEY PUBLISHING COMPANY

Reading, Massachusetts · Menlo Park, California · New York · Don Mills, Ontario
Wokingham, England · Amsterdam · Bonn · Sydney · Singapore
Tokyo · Madrid · San Juan · Paris · Seoul · Milan · Mexico City · Taipei

Many of the designations used by manufacturers and sellers to distinguish their products are claimed as trademarks. Where those designations appear in this book and Addison-Wesley was aware of a trademark claim, the designations have been printed in initial capital letters.

Library of Congress Cataloging-in-Publication Data

Johansen, Robert.
    Upsizing the individual in the downsized organization : managing in the wake of reengineering, globalization, and overwhelming technological change / Robert Johansen and Rob Swigart.
        p.   cm.
    Includes bibliographical references and index.
    ISBN 0-201-62712-4
    ISBN 0-201-48940-6 (pbk.)
    1. Downsizing of organizations. 2. Organizational change—Management. 3. Personnel management. I. Swigart, Robert. II. Title.
    HD58.85.J64   1994
    658.1'6—dc20   94-23154
                                                                        CIP

Cover design by Suzanne Heiser
Text design by Wilson Graphics & Design (Kenneth J. Wilson)
Set in 10-point Palatino by Carol Woolverton Studio

1 2 3 4 5 6 7 8 9-MA-9998979695
Three hardcover printings
First paperback printing, November 1995

Contents

III
REBUILDING AND THE QUEST FOR CONTINUITY

What could be: Creating opportunities for yourself and your
organization, now and in the future
95

Acknowledgments

It was Pascal (and at least a few others) who once apologized for writing a long letter because he didn't have time to write a short one. We had the time and the resources to write a short book. At one stage, we had a manuscript three times the size of the final version, plus a hundred or so graphs and charts. If we haven't gotten it right by now, we have no excuse.

This book was truly a partnership in writing, with many many drafts going back and forth between us. One of us led the way through the first complete draft, with the other following; on the next draft we traded roles, and so on. Hundreds of interviews and many discussions with reviewers spiced the writing process, helping us create and hone the final version. Many people helped us over the course of the past three years.

Our colleagues at the Institute for the Future (IFTF) were constantly supportive and challenging in ways that assisted greatly in our thinking and rethinking. Ian Morrison, president of IFTF, gave us the time and resources to give the book our best effort, and he gave us his ideas at critical junctures. The team members of the Groupware Outlook Project worked with us to track new organizational experiences and new technologies. The outlook team generated a constant stream of ideas that kept us thinking and reactions that kept us rewriting, again and again: Paul Saffo, Andrea Saveri, Mary O'Hara-Devereaux, Jeff Charles, David Sibbet, Harvey Lehtman, Stephanie Bardin, Richard Dalton, Robert Mittman, and Judy Buchan. IFTF's Ten-Year Forecast, now in its seventeenth consecutive year, provided an important background and context regarding business trends and issues. Greg Schmid, leader of this yearly forecasting effort, was particularly helpful. Mari-Pat Boughner offered home-stretch help in focusing and getting our ideas out.

Jennifer Wayne, a serious international researcher in her own right, volunteered to assist us in analyzing data and checking sources. She also reviewed our drafts at various points and made many good suggestions while continually cheering us on.

Many others, including Gary Ireton, Joel Dyar, Marsha Pallitz-Elliott, Don Johnson, and Hans Schwarz, were very helpful to us in developing and expanding our ideas.

Our agent, Rafe Sagalyn, worked with us for months on the initial book proposal, back when its title was "Now That the Buffalo's Gone," referring to the herds of middle managers leaving the corporate prairies. The content thrust that Rafe pulled out of us carries into the final manuscript. Rafe also proposed the title that now appears on the book jacket, while ten pages of other possible titles died in the files of our word processors.

Bill Patrick is our editor at Addison-Wesley, and a better editor we have never known. Somewhere in the second or third of our early chapter drafts, he actually found a few paragraphs he liked. "Write with more steroids!" he challenged. "Go out on a limb!" He was brutal, in a way that was challenging and constructive. He is a writer's editor, perhaps because he is also a writer himself. Many thanks, Bill.

Our families lived through each stage of the manuscript with us, while also helping us draw the line in our work between anytime/anyplace and all the time/everyplace. Special thanks to Robin and Jane, critics and coaches both.

Bob Johansen and Rob Swigart
Menlo Park, California
April 1994

Introduction

This is not a book about corporations; it is a book about people. People left inside larger corporations and government agencies, as well as people on the edges. Especially people on the edges. People like Marco Pellegrini.

One July afternoon Marco looked through the double-paned green glass feeling strangely lethargic, filled with a dread and reluctance to leave his cubicle for the weekly Friday afternoon communications meeting.

Marco is a middle manager in his late forties. He has a wife and child, a boat, a home, a mortgage, and his own department at this highly successful pharmaceuticals firm. But he is uneasy.

"I'd never felt that way before," he says, retelling the story a few weeks later. "The company is in trouble, sure, but that's happened before. This time, it seems to have lost direction, mission."

Marco says that only a few years earlier the company had an enormous cash reserve; it now has a billion-dollar debt. When the stockholders started screaming, the board fired its chairman, and the company reacted by instituting a series of massive layoffs.

Over the years Marco has survived several rounds of such layoffs. The company had a habit of convulsing. People like Marco stayed because they believed it was a good place to work. The benefits were generous, better than industry standards. There was a much-praised culture of tolerance and progressive policies regarding work time, child care, maternity leave, and even periodic sabbaticals for career renewal. There had always been a kind of esprit—at one time a product development group had flown a Jolly Roger over the research building.

Those days are gone. Success has taken some of them, and growth. Flocks of executives entered the company from competing firms, bringing different styles, values, and corporate cultures with them. Lately, with each round of corporate purging and bingeing, Marco has been feeling his time draw close. Whenever managers were laid off, he sensed in the ranks ever-higher levels of anxiety. Even those who remained were running scared.

He finally forced himself to attend the meeting that Friday. "The new president called it a 'communications meeting,' but it's not really a communications meeting anymore; it's got a new format. I'd call it a *broadcast* meeting. We gathered in an auditorium and watched a videotape. The president told us his vision of the company's direction. One way. Broadcast. No questions, no give and take."

Marco takes off his glasses and pinches the bridge of his nose. When he puts the glasses back on he grins. "He ended the so-called meeting by saying, 'There are a lot of people out there with *our* money in their pockets. I want you to go out there and get it.' That kind of crass salesman talk doesn't go over very well with the scientists and product development people, but the president comes from sales." He pauses. "The company's changed. If this keeps up, we'll become nothing. We'll disappear."

Marco means *he* will disappear. "I'm like the turkey who survived Thanksgiving," he says. "It's nice I survived, but Christmas is coming."

Business organizations are changing, whether they want to or not. The changes are chaotic—the experience from inside or close to a large corporation, as well as the feeling inside your stomach. The pyramids of corporate strength have flattened into a web of organizational ambiguity. Individual employees no longer have a sturdy structure to climb. Instead, planning a career is more like crawling out on a webbing of rope, grasping for stability that comes and goes quickly. This is no safety net.

Workers are trading their sense that they'll be taken care of for a realization that they'd better take care of themselves. Job security is a fragile hope that too often becomes a broken promise. And the career path, for a growing number of employees, meanders wildly across a wide range of different corporations, job assignments, and locations.

Making a career has become like making a movie: bring together a team, do the production, disband. Loyalty is not to a single team or a single corporation; teams form and reform, working for a variety of corporate sponsors who commit to tasks, not people. Of course, webs of loyalty form among people who work well together, who then refer each other from one team to the next. This is exciting as long as there is a new team waiting when the old one disbands. It can be exciting for corporations too, as long as there are good people ready to work when a new project begins.

Corporations are going global, reaching out to new markets. On the surface it may seem that they are already global, but this is only half true. Many corporations do function in the global marketplace, but they do so infected with uncertainty and dread about the details of how their work should be done. In fact, global work gets done by people from a crazy quilt of cultures across a maze of distant locations. Travel is only a partial fix, and a regular diet of global travel often leads to a frenzy of disconnection, with little sense of organizational or personal balance. Telecommunications and computing are both part of the solution and part of the problem: they are mandatory for global work, yet there are staggering imbalances in the global electronic infrastructures. Corporations are just beginning to discover which electronic medium is good for what.

It is now possible to do business without buildings. As electronic spaces become more powerful and more flexible, physical places take on a less important role. Virtual spaces become much more significant, for it is here, in nonphysical hyperspace, that buying and selling take place as well as some, much, or all interpersonal exchanges. Office buildings, particularly corporate headquarters, used to be monuments to the stability of the corporations they symbolized. Those beautiful buildings provided comfort for employees, stockholders, customers, and communities. "We're here to stay" was the message they broadcast, speaking for their corporate creators. Now the message from the buildings of corporate America is garbled. Many of the buildings remain, but the confidence does not. Americans still "go to work," but the where, the when, and the how are increasingly open to negotiation.

Meanwhile, "re-words" have invaded the world of business and government: *restructuring, reinvention, redesign, reengineering.* Remarkable—perhaps this is what a recession is really about: an obsession with *re*-words.

The *re*-word preachers, most of whom do not talk with or even know much about each other, have introduced hopeful new visions about how organizations might improve themselves. A few of these new approaches are very good, most are mediocre, and a few are little more than shams. Certainly, the best of them follow practices that are more customized art and skill than they are prepackaged quick fixes.

Even they, however, have thrown up a tangle of terminology and technique. Many of the words they use mean about the same thing; many old methods have been repackaged, with new words to describe them. Bumper sticker thinking only adds to what is already a very confusing time for organizations and the people within them.

For the past five years we have been working closely with people in the midst of corporate restructuring, the beneficiaries of the *re*-words and other attempts to breathe new life into gasping organizations:

acquisitions and mergers; business process redesign; total quality; information systems architectural planning; reengineering. At the Institute for the Future we typically work with managers in middle to senior ranks—the knowledge workers.

We are in the organization for a variety of reasons, but our role is not to do the restructuring. Nonetheless, we have been very close to the process of change. Often we are there at the end of the day, after the *re*-word consultants have gone. The people who are being restructured are our friends as well as our colleagues. We are outsiders to large corporations, but we work closely with the insiders. This gives us an outside-in view, a perspective on what is happening unavailable from the inside.

Amid all the organizational changes of the past few years we became intrigued by the human aftermath of this turmoil. We began collecting stories about people who had gone through organizational changes. We sought out people who had been laid off from large corporations and were forced to create new lives. We talked with many people left inside large corporations after layoffs, restructuring, and reengineering. We talked about their experiences, their hopes, their fears, and what they had learned. These are the human dramas behind the organizational buzzwords.

Upsizing the Individual in the Downsized Organization probes the emerging world of work and the effects it has on the people who are experiencing its dislocations. Part I, "On Shifting Ground: Organizations Today," describes the emerging business world in the wake of reengineering, restructuring, redesign, and their sister processes. We will clarify the new landscape by taking an outside-in look at its most prominent landmarks. Our focus is on people and the organizations that they are creating.

We move in Part II, "Damage Assessment," to our judgments about the characteristics of the emerging organization. This part of the book focuses on the very real hazards of organizational life in the mid-nineties, its dangerous and upsetting ambiguities, why they exist, and where things can go (or are already going) wrong through downsizing, rightsizing, capsizing, and so on. If our organizations continue to evolve as they have been, this section shows what we can expect to see in the future. It isn't pretty.

Part III, "Rebuilding and the Quest for Continuity" sketches an outline of the attitudes, cultural changes, and tools that are necessary for successfully navigating the new organizational frontier, including ways to turn disasters and dislocations into opportunities. To our surprise, some of the saddest people we talked with are those who remain inside, settling in in the reengineered organization and hoping the old days will return. Some of the happiest and most successful people we interviewed were those who left or were laid off and built new lives. They have discovered that there is life after layoff. These few pioneers have already pushed into the wilderness and found it a rich and interesting place.

That wilderness is the future. The middle managers are gone, and they are not coming back. Neither are the corporate monoliths of the past. One interpretation is that the *re*-words and the *re*-word consultants have eaten them alive. But we believe the *re*-words are only part of what is going on. They fall into the same class as the profound but confusing ideas of the media theorist Marshall McLuhan, who was once accused of hitting a very large nail not quite on the head.

The old world has been blown apart. As we'll see—or as you already know all too well—the old boundaries, definitions, job titles, along with the old sense of security, no longer exist. Shaping things to come, technology is now being woven into the organizational structure to fill the gaps. This book assesses the technological fix for the muddle left by downsizing and reengineering. But technology is only a tool, in the way that a hammer is only a tool. Much depends on who is wielding that hammer, which hammer it is, and for what purposes it is being used. This book reminds us all of the importance of the person who selects the tools. Our message, in part, is about new ways of seeing ourselves within this radically different business landscape—new self-definitions, new roles (versus mere job titles), new mind-sets, new metaphors for enhancing performance in the brave new world of work. There are no important job titles left, but there are lots of important jobs.

In his book *Future Perfect*, business visionary Stan Davis has pointed out the danger to organizations in approaching the information economy with mental models drawn from the industrial age.[1] Our goal in this book is to help people find the new images of *themselves* that will allow them to thrive in the emerging environment in which we all must operate.

A new form of organization is struggling to life. It's rough out there, and hanging on to the old mind-set can lead to defeatism and despair. Even in the face of all the pain and confusion, however, opportunities abound.

I

ON SHIFTING GROUND: ORGANIZATIONS TODAY

What is: Fewer managers managing more people with more diversity and more geographic separation but less loyalty to the organization

1

Precursors of
Organizational Change

$\mathbf{W}$e all know the score: mergers and acquisitions have forced organizations to remold themselves in basic ways. Deregulation has had a similar effect on the emergence of new organizational forms. After a merger, traditional hierarchical organizations are often too inflexible to adapt and grow, but the transition has created a crisis in confidence. Those struggling for survival in the midst of this turmoil, and those preparing to enter business, are not prepared for the change.

The origins of this crisis lie in the years after World War II, when the United States looked out over the ruins of Europe and Japan and saw a clear field. Pent-up demand for consumer goods—cars, refrigerators, lawn mowers, popular music recordings—meant American industry could sell anything it could produce. Prosperity was an endless prairie, and corporations expanded almost exponentially to fill those empty spaces.

It took a vast army of managers to control all this growth through the postwar period, youthful, vigorous, dedicated young executives who had come of age in the forties and the optimistic fifties. They had come back from the battlefront brimming with pride and confidence. Their experience managing the war readied them for managing the peace. They felt the tide would continue flowing their way. Their parents, who had come of age in the Depression and expected little of the world, found themselves rewarded beyond anything they could have imagined. The Organization Man of the fifties was promoted to senior executive in the sixties and seventies. This generation formed the bedrock of corporate management, and their children were entering the business world (often with very large corporations) as junior executives—so-called middle managers.

Unlike their parents, these younger executives expected much, having grown up with ever-increasing affluence. They had, in the early sixties, a sense of surfeit, combined with a pride in the precision of American industry. American products were the best in the world. American management was the best in the world. Engineering was the metaphor of the day. Industry was a machine for generating profits, one that could be fine-tuned like an automobile engine.

The Vietnam War changed the metaphor. The principles of management that had worked so well for industry failed miserably when Secretary of Defense Robert McNamara tried to apply them to an unpopular and badly conceived war, the product of a cold war mentality. Vietnam became the new Maginot Line to stop the spread of communism, but the ideological imperatives of the war were vague. There was little coordination between the military and the civilian contractors who were supposed to support them, and little cooperation among the services themselves. Competition, time-serving, jockeying for advantage, and avoiding blame were the new guiding principles.

American attention drifted away from markets. Vast sums were poured into the war, providing incentive for industry to gear up for defense contracting, where getting the job done quickly ruled and efficiency was beside the point.

Meanwhile the Japanese, spending less than half the American percentage of GNP on defense, moved into markets formerly dominated by American business. It was not Pearl Harbor, but it became just as bloody for Americans. This time, they bled green blood.

Then the oil shocks of the seventies further sent American industry reeling. Competition from the more nimble Japanese in automobiles and consumer electronics, the growing threat of the gradually unifying Europe, imbalances in trading policy—all threatened American industry just when it had finally managed to flood the marketplace and was struggling, through constant restyling and heavy advertising pressure, to maintain a market share. There was much talk during that decade of cybernetics, of homeostatic systems and feedback loops, and more middle managers joined the ranks to handle the new complexity and restore America's competitive edge.

At the same time, the rush to business schools began and the leading edge of the baby-boom generation hit the job market. Too many people, a declining economy, and global competition began squeezing the new managerial class. According to Robert Reich, "Between 1976 and 1983, the rate of corporate firings doubled. During the same period, 15 to 25 percent of American executives left their jobs."[1] Although many of these executives left for higher-paying jobs, the pace continued to accelerate throughout the eighties, when "restructuring" left behind a decreasing army of anxious and increasingly cynical managers.

When the *Challenger* space shuttle exploded in 1986, American industry was already deep into a frenzy of leveraged buyouts, mergers and acquisitions, new ways of managing the stress. The *Challenger* disaster was a rude surprise to American management. It revealed serious flaws in the management structure of large projects, especially those touted as cooperative ventures between big government and big business.

Changes in the concept of the corporation were paralleled by changes in the individual's self-concept. In the nineteenth century, for example, the successful individual was the "self-made" man who, through hard work, thrift, pluck, integrity, and perseverance, it was believed, could succeed at anything. He could build a commercial, transportation, or banking empire; he could become president. His values were traditional. He had what was called "character," that mysterious quality, parents exhorted their children, that could only arise from hard work and pain.

After World War II, the self-image of the newly emerging Organization Man was motivated by "personality," the stuff that the grainy black-and-white pictures on television screens in the fifties assured the viewing audience would result from the dedicated use of the right toothpaste and the most effective deodorant—combined with the practiced ability to smile, dance, and make effective small talk.

For the managers of the baby-boom generation, the regulating principle has become the "self,"[2] a man-made construct whose reality is reflected in the self-help and human potential movements of the past twenty years. Indeed, Paul Leinberger and Bruce Tucker's subtitle for this section of their book is "Personal Artifice: From the Self-Made Man to the Man-Made Self."

There are signs that both the nature of organizations and the self-concept of the individuals who make them up are changing in fundamental ways, but it is very difficult, especially from inside the beast, to understand what might be done to direct these changes. We can only say that some fundamental shifts are under way, shifts we explain in more detail in later chapters of this book:

Organizations are evolving from pyramid to fishnet structures as hierarchies collapse and broad, interwoven, flexible structures emerge.

Employees are increasingly turning from dependence on their corporations for health benefits and retirement and career planning to dependence on themselves and networks of co-workers and supporters for these needs.

Businesses have become less preoccupied with outcomes and more focused on process. This basic principle of the total quality movement has been widely adopted, and most large corporations now invest heavily in understanding and improving their business processes.

Within organizations, individuals are less apt to work in big structures and more likely to participate in business teams and ad hoc alliances.

Businesses have shifted their attention from their competitors to their customers. Competitive analysis still plays an important role, but it has been overshadowed by an intense interest in customer needs and customer service. Blind competition is becoming cooperative competition. Companies are becoming sophisticated in identifying those zones where it makes more sense to cooperate than to compete.

Electronic networks are replacing office buildings as the locus of business transactions. You are where your network is; as a corollary, your network is your business.

Diversity is seen less as a problem than as a simple business reality in the global marketplace. Traditional us-versus-them mentality is yielding to the realization that the old majority is becoming a minority—and your customer is often a member of the new majority.

An orientation toward ongoing learning has succeeded one-time training for employees as companies realize that they must have a flexible workforce capable of continually acquiring new skills. Learning must be lifelong, and it's for everyone.

Simplistic notions of linear time ("What have you done for me lately?") are being replaced by a more complex concept that recognizes the need for time management, control of the work flow, and organizational continuity. Time is an intricate dance of multiple cycles, time zones, biological rhythms, and strategies for efficiency. The definition of quality is played out over time.

These shifts are creating enormous ambiguity for those already in the workforce as well as those about to enter the business community. They are scrambling definitions of basic concepts like quality, time, and values. While many of the shifts are mediated by technology (which, in turn, may aid or impede them), the force behind these changes is people and their cultures. Technology is a tool of change, not its cause.

Beginning in the eighties, America's giant corporations began serious reducing, shedding excess organizational weight that, as on a human body, had gathered around the middle. U.S. business went on a diet, and middle managers began to hear terms like "redeployment" (a metaphor borrowed from the military-industrial complex of the time).

By the end of the decade it was clear that size reduction alone was not going to be enough to reinvigorate American business, and the metaphor for business organization changed again. Cybernetic terminology began to fade, coinciding with the loss of U.S. supremacy in the manufacturing of computer processor and memory chips. American business plunged into a series of heroic measures intended to cure what was coming to be a very sick patient. Because increased managerial complexity was producing diminishing returns, corporations began an orgy of reactive medicine. The introduction of "total quality" management techniques imported from Japan, which itself had originally adopted them from American business, was followed by a succession of interventions: downsizing, rightsizing, excessing, overhauling, and so on. Restructuring proceeded on many fronts and under many banners.

By now we have almost lost track of the metaphors that guide our perceptions; we often mistake the map for the territory. Drama, after all, is not real life. Our organizational history and our metaphors shape us profoundly. They help us understand the changes we are experiencing, but they can also confuse us. Today's business metaphors are more prone to confuse than to clarify; they are more part of the problem than they are part of the solution.

Today the self is in a constant process of its own creation. Leinberger and Tucker refer to the "man-made self,"[3] which has its origins in the confluence of much twentieth-century thought. As the human potential movement of the seventies and eighties taught, it is important that we remake our understanding of ourselves whenever the old definition seems to be failing.

Climbing the organizational hierarchy is no longer like climbing stairs in a stable structure. The stairs have become rope ladders, with managers clinging desperately for balance. Organization Man is changing into Spider Woman.

2

Metaphor Management:
Reengineering
and the Rest

Already littered across the business landscape of the nineties are terms like *reengineering, reinventing, restructuring, redesign*—oblique and image-invoking ways of describing change. They are metaphors, figures of speech that describe one thing in terms of something else for purposes of clarification.

The cold war, for example, had nothing to do with temperature; in fact, it had little to do with war. Metaphors are very important when one enters a new area or period; drawing on known, familiar concepts, they help make sense of the unknown. Getting the metaphor right, however, is critical in such situations. An inappropriate metaphor will create unrealistic or unsuitable expectations, but just how may not be known until it is too late to correct them. The rule of thumb for making good use of a metaphor is to compare what is said with what is meant. The trick is not to get confused about which is which.

The domination of *re*-words in today's business world presents a unique set of challenges to understanding. *Re*-words imply, of course, that something has been done in the first place. In order for a company to be reengineered, for example, it would have to have been engineered. The implicit message of a *re*-word is that something has been done before, but now it must be done again. If you want to do something completely new, a *re*-word is not for you.

In 1993 and 1994, business people became entranced by the notion of reengineering. Popularized and even trademarked by Michael Hammer, formerly a professor at MIT, the term became fashionable in 1990 when Hammer published an article introducing the concept in the *Harvard Business Review.*[1] He and James Champy, a consultant for CSC Index, summarized the idea and their early experiences in implementing it in a book that quickly became ubiquitous on airport book racks, just above the self-help section.[2] It was corporate self-help.

The language of reengineering is not subtle. It demands that the leaders of large organizations ask themselves soul-searching questions—fundamental questions such as, What product do we sell that customers will be compelled to buy? How can we reorganize our core processes around that core business? The way Hammer defines it, reeingineering radically changes the business process. "Don't automate, obliterate," he says. True reengineering is not for the faint of heart. It is not casual rethinking, not a simple rearranging of furniture. Predictably, a gulf has arisen between, on the one hand, "real" reengineering as described by Hammer and Champy and as practiced by CSC Index and, on the other, the meaning of the term in popular usage. Although the word *reengineering* dominates business jargon, as a metaphor for organizational change, it has become wildly imprecise.

Likewise, businesses' experiences with reengineering have had mixed results. "In all too many companies, reengineering has been not only a great success, but also a great failure. After months, even years, of careful redesign, these companies achieve dramatic improvements in individual processes only to watch overall results decline."[3]

Reengineering is a mechanical metaphor, with roots in engineering. Is such a metaphor right for the organization of the late nineties?

Peter Keen and Ellen Knapp, who have pointed out the inadequacies of *re*-words and the current focus on reengineering, have developed a more basic approach that emphasizes "getting the right processes right." Whereas the execution of many *re*-word strategies has emphasized slash-and-burn reorganization, Keen and Knapp pose the more positive metaphor of business process "investment" and developing a "process portfolio."[4] And whereas most practitioners of reengineering have emphasized eliminating process costs, Keen and Knapp stress building on process value. Choosing the right metaphor and managing the expectations that result is just as important as the quality of the techniques that are employed.

Why, we might ask, should intelligent people at blue-chip corporations need a metaphor to get themselves to ask basic questions about their own businesses? Perhaps the answer is that the historical changes in the wind are so threatening and ominous that, under their pressure, big corporations easily lose sight of their core competencies and drift into complacency or confusion. Companies must struggle to "get it right" in their business practices. Meanwhile, consultants struggle to get the right metaphor.

If we do not examine our metaphors from time to time, prising out their origins and confirming their utility, they can come to control our thinking. Much misunderstanding in the world originates from the two parts of a metaphor, what is said and what is meant, being confused, especially in the area of religion. More than once in human history people have fought over definitions of such ineffable concepts as God or the Messiah. As Joseph Campbell has said, using the wrong metaphor or taking a metaphor too seriously "may lead to the spilling not only of valueless ink, but of valuable blood."[5]

In the current state of American business, few would deny that blood is flowing. With this dramatic and disorienting shift in the way corporations structure themselves comes a change in business language. Consider the language of certainty used in the sixties, how much more naive it seems in contrast with the less confident words of the business world of the nineties.

1960s	1990s
organize	manage
control	uncertainty
prediction	intuition
plan	coordinate
hierarchy	network
joining	partnering
results	processes
individual	team
opinion	learning
global village	global diversity
the year 2000	the millennium
choices	dilemmas

In the sixties, the word *organize* was an action word that put an emphasis on change and on those who effected it—union organizers, community organizers, organizers of the peace movement, organizers of ecological awareness. Organizers were activists who brought together individuals and ideas to generate enough power to make things happen. Whether they were part of the mainstream culture or the emerging counterculture, they arose from the generation of the Organization Man and were shaped by it.

The Organization Man's dominant survival strategy was to develop "personality." If you had personality, if you were a "people person," you might be a persuader capable of building consensus or talking others into doing something. The manager with personality rose in his organization.

Today the word *organize* seems anachronistic, unless one is speaking of something one might do to a closet. People around the globe are losing the conviction that organizations—governments, the United Nations, corporations—can bring about the changes that were thought to be just over the horizon in the sixties. In the uncertain worlds of our work, social lives, environment, homes, and families, all anyone can do is try to manage—that is, to cope. The dream of the unified global village has given way to the reality of global fragmentation and diversity.

When the structures, institutions, and organizations of the familiar world no longer fulfill people's needs, when the level of uncertainty reaches a threshold, then uncertainty gives way to both threat and opportunity, and change is the only option. It is how one responds that makes the difference, and how one responds depends on how one thinks, including what metaphors one uses.

The word *organization* itself brings the active characteristics of the verb to the static qualities of the noun. Organizations are made up of living people and processes, not things. Their survival depends on how they respond to changes in the external environment. Flexibility is essential; rigid structures do not survive major turbulence. Creating business teams is one visible way organizations have responded to the changing environment.

In the sixties, Americans had implicit faith in technology. Great engineering, it was thought, could solve any problem. The idea of reengineering harkens back to this unquestioned belief that proper engineering would inevitably make things work. "Reengineering" is more a relic of the sixties than a new vision for the nineties.

A very different kind of metaphor for organizational change is Michael Rothschild's notion of "bionomics," which suggests that the evolution of business organizations mirrors the natural evolutionary processes of biology.[6] Economics and biology make strange bedfellows in this metaphor, perhaps, but the result is a very different concept of business, with different incentives, roles, and measures of success. Whether or not one agrees with the details of Rothschild's proposal, he has done a good job of matching his metaphor with his intent.

The biological metaphor gains strength when we think of an organization as being also an *organism*. Corporations have long been considered living entities, accorded the legal rights of a person. They take on identities in our consciousness, with personalities and cultures of their own. But though a corporation is in some ways like a living organism, to call it such is to employ a metaphor.

When we say that a corporation has a personality—that Ben and Jerry's is liberal, say, or that Chase Manhattan is conservative—we are using a metaphor. This perception of the corporation has misled a generation of managers (not to mention investors), who came to believe that a corporation would actually behave like the entity we compare it to in the metaphor.

Corporations feel neither love nor hate; they do not laugh. Unlike individual human beings, a corporation is an artificial mental construct, an abstract, imaginary pattern composed of a brand name, a reputation, an organizational chart, buildings, people, and so on. The organizational model of the sixties is clearly inadequate, and a comprehensive model has yet to appear for the nineties. Many organizations are running blind. We have outlived the usefulness of models from the industrial era but don't yet have robust organizational models for the information era. Unlike Frankenstein's monster, the artificial person of the corporation has never been animated to even a semblance of life. It was a dead image from the beginning—except in the imaginations of row upon row of Organization Men. Certainly it is dead now.

A corporation is more like the pattern of a knot, not the rope; it is the shape energy takes when the human beings who make up an enterprise blend their collective wills, not the human beings themselves. It is people (and in large part those people have been middle managers) who adapt their individual psychologies to a particular pattern, who animate it with the human range of emotions and motives.

In his macro-level analyses of social change, Stan Davis has argued that solid organizational models do not usually appear until near the end of an economic era.[7] The convincing models for the industrial economy, for example, were developed only in the twenties and thirties, just as the industrial era was ending.

Many businesses today still use the organizational models of the industrial era to understand the new information economy. To describe the vision of electronic connection on a national or global scale, for instance, the best that Washington visionaries could come up with is the concrete metaphor of an "information highway" to describe a phenomenon that doesn't have anything like the look and feel of a road. The Internet is the first manifestation of the so-called information highway. It is a complex network of networks, growing organically and in ways that are very difficult to understand, particularly if you use the wrong metaphor. Those who best understand the Internet are engineers who grasp its underlying technology. It is more like a termite mound or a mushroom patch than a highway system.

For the information economy, Davis suggests, "we can expect capstone managerial models to appear on the scene around 20 years from now, plus or minus a decade—that is, around 2010, and certainly not before the end of the century."[8] Such models, like those of the industrial era, will provide clear guidelines for structuring work in the information era.

Like the word *organization, planning* was also dominant in the sixties and seventies. Planning is the search for control, and there was a strong sense of urgency about getting things under control.

Clients of the Institute for the Future during the seventies had titles like "vice president for corporate strategic planning." Such titles are now rare. Corporations still make plans, of course, but it is typically a line-business responsibility. Planning has descended to the realm of the middle manager. Central corporate groups are smaller, and they tend to coordinate rather than initiate, coach rather than command. Planning is more responsive than active. Corporations coordinate their responses, trying to manage uncertainty. Often, it seems, organizations are attempting to manage the unmanageable. As Peter Keen has argued, "the challenge for a firm is how to plan when it cannot predict."[9]

Meanwhile, erratic economies worldwide, radically changing skill levels in the workforce, a dizzying mix of traditional and nontraditional workers, highly competitive global markets, and unceasing advances in technology challenge traditional organizational structures. A rising chorus calls for radical change.

It is important to manage your metaphors, to understand both their potentials and limits. As Ed Artzt, former CEO of Procter and Gamble, said after announcing a round of restructuring and layoffs, "We're not banking on things getting better with time. We're banking on us getting better."[10] He understood where the emphasis of his metaphor lay, and how to manage the change. People, not things, improve an organization.

Metaphors abound. It's a jumble out there. Picking the right metaphor is critical.

3

The Fishnet

Organization

All the many forces of organizational change are having one major seismic effect: they are flattening the corporate structure. Hierarchies haven't gone away, but they are changing in fundamental ways. The old, stable pyramid shape, with a broad base of line workers, a medium range of middle managers, and a few top executives, is gone. What replaces the monolithic corporation is what we call the fishnet organization.

Imagine a net laid out on a dock. If you grab a node and lift, the rest of the net lattices nicely under it. A temporary hierarchy appears as long as you hold up the node, with layers consistent with how high you lift the node and the width of the mesh. The hierarchy disappears when you lay the net down. Pick up another node, another soft hierarchy appears. Any node can connect with any other, in three dimensions. (See Figure 3-1.)

The fishnet is a metaphor we chose to express the form of organization emerging from the current turmoil. If we are correct that tomorrow's organizations will function like fishnets, it is important to think of them, talk about them, and create them like fishnets. If we hire pyramid builders, mechanics, or road builders to create an organizational fishnet, the results will be disappointing. Fishnets are not made of wood, steel, or concrete. Unfortunately, many of today's corporate organizations are still being built by people who think they are building rigid structures. Their metaphors, and therefore their tools, are wrong.

The pursuit of control that characterized the sixties was consistent with the hierarchical organizations of the late industrial era. Strength was equated with rigidity. The belief that hierarchical organizational

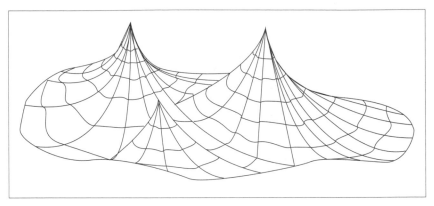

Figure 3-1   Organizational structures are beginning to look like fishnets

structure makes for good business is a difficult one to give up. Gradually, though, hierarchy is giving way to more horizontal structures with complex yet flexible webs of interconnection.

Many organizations still lack such structures. Day-to-day operations continue, and most people still believe that leaders at the top of large companies determine the organization's direction. Senior executives, so the belief goes, direct things with a firm, steady, and omniscient hand. This assumption is increasingly suspect. In fact, many senior executives admit that they have considerably less control over their organizations than most people think, and the word is spreading through the ranks. There is nobody at the helm of the corporate ship, because there is no helm. Managers do have an effect, but they are pulling and rearranging fishnets.

Traditional organizations have established nodes: key people, permanent roles, departments, and basic structures, but such structures are relatively inflexible. The fishnet is flexible; it can form and re-form varied patterns of connection. The middle manager may at one time be at the apex, at another in the middle. The fishnet organization rearranges itself quickly while retaining its inherent strength.

As we move ahead in the nineties and beyond, fishnet structures will become increasingly attractive. Hierarchies will come and go in most organizations, but many other informal structures will arise to meet immediate demands and achieve long-term flexibility. Richard Nolan of the Harvard Business School refers to such structures as "informal networks floating on hierarchies."[1] Sometimes the informal networks are business teams. At other times an independent consultant (most likely a former middle manager) may find herself more inter-

16

ested in the web of networks in which she participates than in the corporate hierarchy underlying it.

Teams, not hierarchies, do the real work. The traditional hierarchy will have only a local, limited, internal role. The underlying organizational structure (the fishnet) should have visible form, like the strong rope or cord that holds the net together. But informal, ad hoc networks may then appear and disappear as the net is rearranged.

Information technologies, including a combination of telecommunications and computing, are the cord out of which the organizational fishnet is woven. Dictionary definitions suggest that the word *network* has the same functional sense whether it is applied to electronic or organizational networks, although nontechnical people especially tend to view the word as having more a technological than a social or organizational meaning. The idea of a fishnet is similar to that of a network, but it characterizes the structure of the new work environment in a more flexible, more organic way. The down-to-earth fishnet metaphor humanizes the abstract concept of an electronic network of connections, the network that actually makes the connections for our organizations.

New organizational charts often look like wiring diagrams for networks. The "network organization," as described by Raymond Miles and Charles Snow, is increasingly practical.[2] Most of us already work within interconnected structures that are based on projects or teams. Electronic networks can support this organizational structure by providing the primary means of connection. If electronic nets can be brought to life by an effective social and managerial process, they can provide flexible yet strong links for organizations.

The fishnet is not a pipe dream of tomorrow, but an emerging reality of today. One example demonstrating this is that of Asea Brown Boveri, an electrical systems and equipment manufacturer employing more than 240,000 people around the world and having annual revenues of more than $25 billion. Though it is coordinated at the central level and retains definite elements of hierarchical integration, the company gives its individual nodes great freedom. Characterizing the corporation's innovative structure, CEO Percy Barnevik says: "We want to be global and local, big and small, radically decentralized with centralized reporting and control. If we resolve these contradictions, we create real organizational advantage."[3]

ABB is composed of small regional work units that function like independent businesses, led by a strong central executive committee that oversees and tracks performance and makes quick decisions if

17

needed. The executive committee is comprised of the four heads of product segments, who are responsible for product efficiency; the three heads of the three global regions, the Americas, Europe, and the Asia-Pacific region; and the company CEO, who is based in Zurich. The level below the executive committee is made up of the heads of the national offices, who are responsible for customer services, government relations, and sales strategies. The regional work units constitute the third and lowest level.

This structure allows the executive committee to exert control and continuity, while the decentralized units allow for flexibility and response to uncertainty. The net is thus cast wide. It has the ability to respond to local conditions, and the flexibility to adapt.

Most organizations have no choice about whether or not to take part in this real-life experiment in creating the fishnet organization of tomorrow. There may be a good case for caution regarding how fast to move toward a fishnet structure, but it is dangerous to hang back.

The fishnet organization is made up of individuals forged into small, ad hoc, cross-organizational, time-focused, task-driven work groups, usually called teams. The key trait of teams, the basic structural unit of the fishnet organization, is their ability to put numbers on the board quickly. Teams mean action and bureaucratic bypass.

But the strength of teams is also their weakness: teams don't scale up to teams of teams very well unless specific and unusual efforts are made. It is possible, indeed likely, that individual teams within a larger organization can perform well on their own, yet be out of sync with each other, in which case the overall organization can fail. The whole can easily be less than the sum of the parts; the sum of separate high-performing teams is not necessarily a high-performing organization. Individual teams can succeed while contributing to their parent organization's failure.

Team members feed on their own adrenaline. The groups can function like political campaigns or professional sports teams, carrying their own psychic rewards. But structures for coordinating the activities of teams of teams are tough to build, and even tougher to maintain. Indeed, hot teams tend to be susceptible to us-versus-them thinking.

Flexible fishnet structures are dependent on teams. Businesses large and small are rapidly forming and re-forming themselves into a complex, ever-shifting set of relationships among individuals and the bewildering array of temporary and permanent corporate entities, partners, and alliances that employ them. This chaotic mix, which Kenichi Ohmae calls the "interlinked economy," is spreading around the globe, mingling cultures, consumer desires, resources, and knowledge across national, linguistic, and ethnic borders.[4] The flow of finance and information dances fleet-footed over time zones and governmental constraints. The interlinked economy has taken on life and energy of its own making. It cannot be stopped, but it can stop the unwary or the unprepared.

The players in the interlinked economy are actually teams of teams, playing against other teams of teams. Many team members are on more than one team. The battle lines are not at all clear: a competitor may also be an alliance partner. A sometimes-creative confusion reigns at the teams-of-teams level.

Despite this disorder, business teams are the only viable organizing unit in such a climate since they can be configured quickly and thrown immediately into full operation. Formed correctly of the right people, teams are flexible and responsive. The gamble from a company's perspective is whether or not the right people will be available as needs or opportunities arise to form new teams. The gamble for prospective team members is whether they will be ready for the call when it comes, or likely to get the call in the first place.

The secret to getting good people when you need them is, of course, to offer them rewards. But how, in all this exciting but unsettled (and unsettling) activity, can companies satisfy employees? How can knowledge workers in this environment ever feel adequately rewarded when there is no one person, nor even one locus of authority, to confer such recognition? If a corporation is its people, as executive visionaries have taught us, what happens if the people are a people in flux? Even if individual team members do feel rewarded and fulfilled, how do you get them to cooperate with other teams and teams of teams, some members of which they will not know and may not understand or even like?

Teams are likely to be geographically dispersed and culturally diverse. Their members may have different professions, different beliefs, different sets of skills. But because they are dispersed, they have remote sensors in many locations. Their overlapping skills not only allow them to respond to problems but also create them.

At the simple end of the spectrum, a team may be the entire fishnet structure. Within that structure, an individual may be a member of several teams at the same time, with different hierarchical functions on each one, different levels of responsibility, different tasks. But such organizational simplicity is rare. A team is more likely to be only a portion of the fishnet, which is itself a team of teams.

In the topsy-turvy world of teams and teams of teams, economies of scale are giving way to economies of structure. The logic of business organization developed in the industrial age emphasized the virtues of increasing size. Just as size offered advantages for the great dinosaurs of the Mesozoic era, size gave corporations of the industrial era benefits that boosted their productivity. It allowed them to purchase more supplies at better prices. It allowed them to scale up manufacturing processes for greatest efficiency. It allowed them to control the avenues of distribution, and to muscle out those who opposed them. It allowed consumers access to cheaper goods because of what came to be called "economies of scale." Big was beautiful.

In the nineties, straightforward mass production is a thing of the past, although what Stan Davis calls "mass customization" still has economic value since it combines big and small in ways that are attractive to customers.[5] Now the structure a company creates for itself, its flexibility and responsiveness, shape its ability to adapt and thrive. Just being bigger is not enough. Size is a virtue only when it is combined with flexibility.

Big is unwieldy, awkward, and slow to respond. Big is laborious and deliberate. For the last twenty-five years, the major corporations in the United States have been getting smaller. Certainly, the recent waves of restructuring have speeded up the decline, but this is a long-term trend. *Fortune* magazine has noted that "IBM, General Motors, and Sears were stars in total market value in 1972, but after two decades they were conspicuously absent from the Big 20."[6] In the end, size didn't work for the dinosaurs either.

The pace of innovation and change is increasing. Computer technologies have allowed manufacturers to develop mass customization, to take orders, program assembly lines, and turn out products in record time. Toyota, for example, can produce a made-to-order automobile in seventy-two hours. Goods can be varied slightly and repackaged for local markets throughout the world. Different, yet similar; global, but local. A flexible structure, with local authority to respond to customers and suppliers through rapid, Delta Force response teams, will beat a slow leviathan every time.

Economies of structure mean that cheaper is now also faster to market, faster with innovation, faster with coordination, faster with customer service. Economies of organizational structure is a new game, though, played by new rules. Managers who understand only economies of scale will be using the wrong metaphor at the wrong time.

4

From Workplace
to Work Space

The physical buildings and the electronic infrastructure of office work are evolving rapidly, along with new organizational forms. People need to work together, but there is no inherent need for the links among them to form inside an office building.

This means the traditional office *building* (not just the office) is changing its shape. Individuals can work anywhere: at home, on airplanes, in hotel rooms, in automobiles, even on the golf course. Cellular phones, modems and faxes, laptop computers and software to integrate working groups are already here, weaving disparate groups of people into virtual corporations. Packaging of such systems for the home has improved dramatically. It is now possible to equip home, neighborhood office, train, bus, boat, bicycle, or automobile for global communications. Of course, today's equipment is still very awkward and crude. The modern road warrior carries a dizzying array of tools just to deal with the variety of hostile environments he is likely to encounter. The situation is improving, but pioneers must be a hearty breed.

Stan Davis calls this phenomenon the "anytime/anyplace economy," which enables businesses to respond to customer demands or competitive pressures without regard to office hours or geography.[1] The anytime/anyplace office means that members of teams can experience a sense of freedom from the physical office, with its physical barriers between workers. Physical offices are vaporizing into "virtual offices" that spring into being wherever and whenever needed and disappear as quickly.

The technology supporting business teams has created a range of options for employees working together. "Groupware" is now practical for many businesses. "Computer-supported collaborative work" (CSCW) allows serious academic inquiry and research. Groupware assists in face-to-face meetings, coordinates teams of teams in large corporations, and filters the most important nuggets from reams of complex information. Electronic tools linking geographically separated teams have eased constraints on teamwork. Most of these electronic tools help teams do what they did before, only faster and better.

A Texaco conference room in Houston, for example, includes a U-shaped table with a workstation for each participant, a video teleconferencing connection to many sites around the world, and a display system for shared organizational memory. Participants can use multiple media from the same point of access as the need arises. People around the globe in the 142 countries where Texaco has a presence can tap into such resources.

But to work over time and spatial distance, team members must communicate through some medium. Increasingly this communication occurs not in workplaces, but in work *spaces*. Both within and outside the corporation, managers may want the familiarity of face-to-face meetings as well as the flexibility of different times/different places or anytime/anyplace communications.

Whether their work space is real or virtual, businesses must provide easy, convenient access to a wide range of electronic media from varied locations, at varied times, for varied users. These media must support basic work activities: communications (to build on connections via telephone and electronic mail), coordination (to assist people in working together and exchanging information), and group support (to facilitate joint work, within teams and across the enterprise).

An office is not merely a building but a complex collection of very human processes. In fact, it need not have a defined physical space at all. This is especially true for those in entrepreneurial enterprises. The emerging electronic options for office activities, such as meeting and work-flow support, group scheduling, project management, messaging, and group writing, all contribute to productivity. The anytime/anyplace office, a virtual space, has moved out of the corporate building and into the world at large. It is where anytime/anyplace business is done.

Many, perhaps most, people will work anytime/anyplace not because they want to, but because that's what their companies require of them. The public image of telecommuting has been dominated by cottage cuteness. In the typical scene, upscale professionals happily tote the gadgets that embody their electronic offices to Santa Fe or Lake Tahoe, followed closely by news photographers writing stories about telecommuters. Telecommuting is now reaching the mass market, where it is not as picturesque but has more practical value.

As we get closer to the millennium, Americans will think of companies less as buildings and more as processes and products. Not only will business managers work in new spaces away from traditional office buildings, but they will work at any time, not just during the traditional eight-hour business day. This is the brave new world of remote work.

Telecommuting (coined by visionary researcher Jack Nilles in 1973) did not become practical on a large scale until the mid-eighties. Managers have been resistant, but there has been a strong latent demand for telework. Simple substitution of automobile commuting by exclusive work from home has not happened much at all. But there are many variants of telecommuting that are practical.

In the mid-eighties, aggressive forecasts for the rapid growth of telecommuting were common in the industry press. The late eighties were a period of I-told-you-so criticisms of these forecasts. A general feeling spread among businesspeople that telecommuting had been tried and hadn't worked. In fact, simple technology is all that is needed for most forms of telecommuting.

Anytime/anyplace capabilities add dimension to fishnet organizations. Telecommunications is the flexible cord connecting organizations on the move. The anytime/anyplace option gives flexibility to the organization, providing the links among its nodes.

The number of jobs that can be done from anywhere is growing. A U.S. government study of the 800-number catalogue merchandising business concluded with the rallying phrase: "In the mail-order business, *wherever there's a phone, there's a job.*"[2] We may question what kind of job it is and who would want it, but it is a job.

Nilles estimates that 70 percent of the information workers in the United States (about fifty million Americans) could work remotely at least part of the time.[3] He estimates that there are about 9 million telecommuters in the United States already. The researcher, who first began working with his model in 1974, has released new forecasts of telecommuting growth using different scenarios. The "business as usual" scenario, which assumes a gradual growth in telecommuting, would result in an annual savings of 50 billion passenger-miles, or 1.2 billion gallons of gasoline, by the year 2000. Under the "high acceptance" scenario, characterized by a combination of more extreme factors such as environmental crisis, rapid change in consumer habits, regulatory pressures, war, or other major events, about 163 billion passenger-miles and 4 billion gallons of gasoline would be saved.[4]

As corporations decrease long-term commitments to their employees on things like health care, retirement, and incentives for lifelong employment and come to rely more on temporary workers, competitive pressures are pushing them into offering more flexible work options in order to recruit quality employees, who often find variations of anytime/anyplace business attractive.

Pacific Bell, another early experimenter with telecommuting, has made its pilot program permanent. As one manager comments, "What counts in telecommuting has more to do with the person than the task. A successful telecommuter is a self-starter who does not require interaction with colleagues or management, and who has a special task to accomplish."[5] Individual initiative is even more important when the worker is part of an outsource web.

Government is also involved in pioneering the telecommunications workplace. The California Telecommuting Pilot, a state project begun in 1987 that includes a careful documentation of costs and benefits, has received very positive evaluations. State employees worked an average of 6.5 days a month via telecommunications in 1989. Moreover, the number of days per month employees worked at remote sites increased with experience. Work, home, and regional telework centers are under development in California, with strong support from both the legislature and regulatory agencies. The pilot met or exceeded its criteria for success in all categories: telecommuter work effectiveness; enhancements in quality of life; results-oriented management techniques; procedures for selection, training, and evaluation of telecommuters; and potential for reducing traffic congestion, air pollution, and energy use.[6] The City of Los Angeles has experienced similar results and has recently voted to extend telecommuting to 15,000 of its 44,000 employees.

Companies like Texaco are realizing that the clock is ticking on the Clean Air Act requirements. By 1995, they must reduce commuters' driving time by 25 percent. This is a huge amount: cutting the workweek to four days would result in only a 20 percent reduction in commuting. To make the goal without using telecommuting facilities, employees at one Texaco site in Houston would need to carpool on an unprecedented scale, averaging four riders per vehicle.

The early indications from Texaco's recently completed telecommuting pilot program are very promising, and a permanent effort may soon be under way. The project calculated that the costs of equipping and supporting telecommuters would be recovered within five years, beyond which there would be a net reduction in operating costs, which seems very conservative. All this is happening in a corporate culture where work from home has been rare.

Besides legislative and business forces, nature plays a role as well. The Los Angeles earthquake of January 1994, for example, was a signal event. Earlier earthquakes had encouraged companies in California to increase their use of remote work, but that of 1994 did more damage to L.A.'s freeway system than ever before, and there were better electronic tools available to help remote workers get set up. If a significant number of commuters in Los Angeles can be kept out of their cars and off the roads, it can happen anywhere. As Bob Metcalfe, inventor of the networking standard called Ethernet and now publisher of the computer trade magazine *Infoworld*, commented at a conference recently, "Wire up your homes and stay there."

Such forays into the new world of anytime/anyplace business remind us, though, that offices have a significance beyond the physical space and technological support they provide. They have always been more than mere places to work; they are also symbols. Creating a clear boundary between work and home, they visibly, tangibly signal status and authority. The work space assigned to an individual employee acquires a history that promotes a sense of continuity. The changing of the name on the brass plate on the door offers proof of personal worth: when another worker moved up the ladder to a better office, you got her old one. The office confers a sense of self-worth; it can be a reward for a job well done. It gives evidence of the approval of peers and keeps one in contact with the traditions of the past. The higher a worker rises, the nicer the office. Ironically, the best are often reserved for those who travel the most. Even the rarely occupied office, however, is a symbol of accomplishment.

As the organizational environment changes, people are trying to recapture or re-create these talismans of connection and self-worth. One factory automation company, for example, has taken to outfitting oak roll-top desks with electronic tools needed on the factory floor. Such furnishings, they think, provide status for users of the systems and make them feel more at ease. Such considerations of human comfort will continue to be important in the anytime/anyplace office. (See Figure 4-1.)

The rise of the fishnet organizational structure means that fewer people will have traditional offices on corporate sites, but the need for

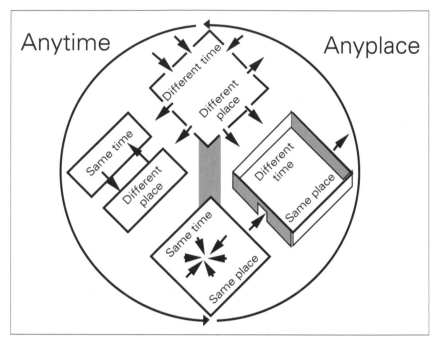

Figure 4-1 The basic meeting options for fishnet organizations

symbols of status and belonging will remain, and even increase. What will the symbols of success be in the virtual office?

For some employees, the computer they carry will be symbolic. The tools and personalized aids on the virtual desktop will provide a sense of location and strength. Some teleworkers now have pictures of their families scanned in to their computers, which can be displayed on the corner of the screen, just like a picture on a desk. A worker traveling in a foreign country, stuck in an overcrowded airport, or alone in a cramped hotel room can gain comfort from seeing the same images that are on the home desktop screen. The employee is not alone; he is valued back at the home office. It's just that the home office isn't there anymore.

George Radcliffe works for a large clothing manufacturer in which he has risen to the rank of vice president, with a corner office, his name on the door in brass, authority over those below him in the hierarchy. When the company decided to reengineer, George's corner office became a meeting room. His new office is a cubicle in the center of the building, without a door, a window, or a secretary.

"It was strange at first," he says. "But I must admit that it is a better use of my old office space; it gives everyone meeting in there a view. The old status symbols have been replaced with others, I guess. A sense of adventure, perhaps? Isn't that a reward in itself? I miss the old trappings, sure, but I'm excited about the changes."

George's cubicle is still a symbolic office, a psychologically comforting place that identifies him as an important contributor to his team and his company—a leader, in fact. He reassures himself with the thought that, like Japanese business leaders, he sits in the middle of the room, with others clustered closely around. In Japan, "window sitters" are those left outside the action; though they have no essential role, they are kept on, paid to look out the window because of the cultural tradition of long-term employment, because of the aversion to laying people off. Window sitters have nothing to do but sit. George keeps reminding himself that he's in the heart of the action.

Of course, many companies still have closed offices with a view, but the tide is turning. The norm for knowledge work is shifting in the fishnet anytime/anyplace organization. The symbolic office is becoming more abstract and ethereal, rather than physical and overt. It is, however, no less important. In most companies today, what is most obvious is the absence of the old symbols rather than the presence of new ones. Anxiety is in the air. Where work will be done should not be an assumption; it is a question that must be asked. The many possible answers are out on the frontiers of change, dramatic change.

5

Diversity plus
Distance

George Radcliffe's new responsibilities have confronted him with situations he never encountered before. "I go into meetings now and the old hierarchy is flattened. I don't have the kind of authority I did before. My team has to exchange ideas and information with other teams, people who used to be well below me in the hierarchy. People who are different from me. And I have to listen—we all do."

George finds himself talking and listening to women and minority workers, people with educational levels and cultures different from his own. It's been a stretch for him. He's had to overcome old habits and old attitudes.

The new diversity of the business world encompasses a wide range of differences. In a country as diverse as the United States, most everyone is different in one way or another. This is especially true in California, where non-Hispanic whites now make up only 55 percent of the population. Mothers of young children continue to enter the workforce, bringing with them their special needs. Immigrants from Latin America and Asia further complicate the employment picture. Issues of gender, ethnicity, sexual preference, physical handicaps, professional expertise, age, religion, and language are helping to shape the evanescent organisms that new and reborn organizations are becoming.

Many people in the diverse workforce are members of teams; many are telecommuters, visible only as names in a telecommunications network and not physically present. Delicacy and tact are required for employees in this anytime/anyplace workforce. A high percentage of telephone operators are black, for example, but only a very small proportion of dental hygienists are. Asked in a survey to explain the relatively small number of African Americans in dental hygiene, dentists revealed the racism underlying this fact. Astoundingly, they reported that "white patients do not want black fingers in their mouths."[1]

Telephone operators, by contrast, work at a distance. The color of their skin, the shape of their bodies, their taste in clothing—all are irrelevant to their ability to do their job (although language and accent can be an issue). They are workers in an anytime/anyplace business.

Diversity may seem to be less of an issue when employees have this distance, but business teams cross other terrain. Members of a single team often belong to different professions, each with its own culture. They may be marketers and engineers, salespeople and financial officers, production specialists and corporate communicators. Professions, like nationalities, have cultures, and sometimes their biases make communication difficult.

Workforce diversity is being stirred into the global environment of anytime/anyplace business. Teams form over national boundaries and across multiple time zones. Meanwhile, the time available for projects is growing shorter. Teams are expected to produce while juggling all the factors of working across distances that are both spatial and temporal.

Telemarketers, telephone operators, and catalogue order takers may work at home. Their contact with the public is mediated by electronic technology, but they are also dealing with diversity at a distance. Their interaction with others requires the same skills as those of business team members. People are learning new modes of courtesy and communications to help smooth this process.

Residual racism must erode under the time and space pressures of such distanced diversity. The diverse world is shrinking and all of us, whatever our color, gender, sexual orientation, age, and physical condition, are pressed into closer contact. Our work requires cooperation, although the roots of diversity remain. Under these conditions, workers are constantly challenged to relearn tolerance and understanding along with other new skills.

We are entering an era of distance and diversity on a global scale. For example, at any given moment there are over three hundred thousand people *in the air* over the United States alone, a virtual flying city. Tourism is already a dominant industry sector worldwide. Youth culture covers the globe, and teenagers in Paris identify with teenagers in Tokyo more readily than they identify with their parents. There are over five hundred contractors from all parts of the world working on the new Boeing 777 aircraft. This is diversity and distance on an unprecedented scale.

6

Just-in-Time
Everything

In the interlinked, transglobal, cross-temporal economy, with its babble of diverse languages and the speed of its technological and cultural change, training is obsolete almost as soon as it is completed.

Companies have always trained new employees. Telephone operators would be hired and put through a weeklong training course, where they learned company policy and procedure and the skills needed for the job. After that it was all on-the-job training, or no training at all.

The popularity of books such as Peter Senge's *The Fifth Discipline: The Art and Practice of the Learning Organization* indicates a growing interest in new approaches to learning.[1] Even so, companies are just beginning to understand how to create a true learning organization. Senge's book has become an icon for interest in organizational learning. But despite the executive rhetoric about the need for training and continuous learning, corporate investment in training in the United States is actually going down, from $52 billion in 1989 to $45 billion in 1992.

Linking individual employees to sources of knowledge outside the organization is also common. The number of electronic bulletin board systems and special-interest distribution lists set up within professional or industry bodies has skyrocketed recently. Searches on the Internet reveal that there were thirty-five hundred new user groups in August of 1993, and estimates range from forty-five hundred to nine thousand in March of 1994, though it is currently impossible to separate professional from fringe groups.

Many workers now outside the corporation are using bulletin boards as electronic "invisible colleges." Such sources of learning help fill the gaps for employees in the new, leaner organization who have fewer co-workers in their field. The boards provide a sense of balance for this generation of more loosely connected workers, who feel greater loyalty to their own disciplines than to the company, and therefore value these contacts more highly than before.

As product cycles gain speed, learning (a graduate degree, for example) once and for all for a career is no longer a truly viable life plan. Learning, like training, quickly becomes obsolete. The new mode is to learn when the learning is needed, not to count on learning in advance.

Lifelong learning is still more vision than reality, however, even though it is well on its way to becoming a necessity. As yet, it is a need few corporations or individuals know how to satisfy. The transition from training to learning involves more than managers putting Senge's book out on their desks.

"Just in the nick of time" used to be a tag line for last-minute rescue jobs, many of which were monuments to bad planning. Companies are now marshaling planning resources to institutionalize last-minute rescues, just in time.

Learning is only one kind of just-in-time activity. There are many others. The business trends of the past decade have emphasized the necessity for more timely operations. Reengineering offered a technical fix for what were seen as lapses in the smooth operation of ongoing business processes.

American automobile companies, for example, used to maintain large inventories of spare parts, both for the automobiles they were making and the assembly line machinery itself, because the parts were often defective and the assembly lines often broke down. By integrating parts manufacturing with assembly and bringing assembly line workers into the process, Toyota challenged American practice, producing nearly defect-free parts for both automobiles and the assembly line. Making defects in automotive parts and assembly line breakdowns rare, the company then instituted a program of just-in-time inventory, freeing resources that used to be spent on fixing glitches for the process of production itself.

Besides inventory, just-in-time planning is being applied to manufacturing, design, distribution, sales, service, even budgeting. The implicit belief that pervades just-in-time logic is simple: the future is so uncertain that the best you can do is to be prepared for any type of last-minute rescue. Just in the nick of time.

With the growing speed of communications, product development, manufacturing, and distribution—with instantaneous electronic transfer of documents, drawings, and specifications, overnight shipment of parts to anywhere in the world, even delivery of fresh-frozen fish within a day to the most remote inland restaurant—the issue of quality is increasingly important. There is neither time nor room for mistakes. The information era is thus bringing about a remarkable and potentially profound reorientation of quality improvement.

Time compresses, but quality expands. Quality improvement programs are management programs of wide scope that seek to orchestrate the usually separate components of a business into one integrated whole. In addition to their focus on quality, most of these programs also have another common theme: they tend to take an enterprise-wide view of business activities.

The late W. Edwards Deming, Joseph Juran, Phil Crosby, and Genichi Taguchi have been the most visible proponents of what is known as the total quality movement.[2] Quality consultants, however— their advice itself of varied quality—abound. Information systems are introducing similar quality improvement programs to link information systems with basic business needs. Most of the Big Six accounting firms now offer trademarked programs, following the lead of several independent firms and business school researchers. Quality improvement programs get managers to think about the future, allowing them to reexamine basic assumptions about their businesses, including relationships with suppliers and customers.

Many *Fortune* 500 companies have large-scale quality efforts under way. Most programs share five basic characteristics. They

focus on customers;

are holistic and take a systemic view;

emphasize process, not outcomes;

drive decisions by data; and

have a long-term orientation.

Business teams are critical to implementing total quality programs. In fact, we might argue that the current trend to improve quality among U.S. businesses is fueled by the trend toward business teams, and vice versa. Quality is elusive, and the flexible organization must be fast on its feet in pursuit of quality goals. The total quality framework can provide long-term continuity as an overarching ideal that balances the ad hoc immediacies common to business teams.

Florida Power and Light (FPL) is generally viewed as one of the early U.S. success stories in total quality training. FPL followed a planning process with both top-down and bottom-up characteristics to arrive at a very short list of long-term objectives (what the Japanese call *hoshins*) that everyone can agree to and keep focused on. One such *hoshin*, for example, was "to reduce the frequency and duration of electric outages to Western Division customers." With managers all concentrating on the same desirable end state, a set of prescribed procedures aligned current activities to the long term.

Total quality programs continue to be on an upswing worldwide, though the jury is still out on their effectiveness, and their popularity has recently waned in the United States. The programs emphasize developing a shared language and common techniques for analyzing and interpreting data. According to Deming, it can easily take five years for the benefits of such a program to be discernible in a large company. The companies most likely to succeed in their efforts at quality improvement are those whose survival is threatened by outside forces.

Certainly, the underlying values of quality programs are consistent with the needs of fishnet organizations. An interest in quality is here to stay, even though quality programs may not be the best way to deliver this message. Quality may be too important to leave to total quality consultants; it is everyone's business, everyone's concern. The quest for quality is continuing, but the best means of achieving it are debatable.

The shifts discussed in Part I are resulting in dislocation, downsizing, job loss, and uncertainty in the global business world. The proliferation of job search programs organized by clubs, professional associations, and business organizations is only the most visible manifestation of more profound problems underlying all the glitz of organizational change and the gloom of shattered careers.

The changes in the U.S. business environment have created numerous potential problems that will only worsen without attention. In the reengineered business world, fewer managers direct more employees, who are more diverse in their traits, more scattered geographically, and less loyal to the organization than ever before. Such a world is inherently unstable, and its structures cannot last.

II

DAMAGE ASSESSMENT

What would be: Why this emerging organizational
structure won't work in the future

7

Problems with

Fishnet Organizations

During the Vietnam War, the United States bombed, mined, and defoliated the Ho Chi Minh Trail. Strategists viewed the trail as an interstate highway, a monolithic artery that could be severed. This metaphor misled U.S. policymakers. The Ho Chi Minh Trail wasn't a highway; it was a fishnet with a pattern the Americans couldn't understand. It was a tangled web of paths, roads, and tracks through wilderness. It could not be cut or blocked.

Currents of organizational change are like that, especially now that the middle managers are all but gone. We may block or steer a tributary here, a branch there, but the flow cannot be stopped. The vacuum left by middle management has made way for a revolution, and the course toward the future is more like the Ho Chi Minh Trail than a reengineered superhighway (information or otherwise). Just as individual Vietnamese pushed bicycles and carried small amounts on their backs along the trail, together creating a human torrent, individuals in the emerging business organization are creating new ways of working.

Fishnet organizations are inherently unstable and unpredictable. This is both their strength and their weakness. Their very flexibility creates an uncomfortable ambiguity for those who are part of them. Responsibility trickles down to every individual; no one seems to be in charge. People may begin wondering, Am I doing a good job? How do I know? What constitutes success? Employees may then come to resist the kinds of changes that are under way today.

We see the results of this resistance in those who grasp desperately for comforting forms, for the trappings and rituals of righteous religions or extremist political agendas, or any of a smorgasbord of self-help formulas: therapies, quick fixes, neoprimitive support groups, twelve-step programs, one-size-fits-all, single-issue programs for change. If they do not recover quickly and move on, these people will be left behind by others with more flexibility, more tolerance for uncertainty, and more capacity for accepting and even anticipating change.

The questions of the fallen middle managers, however, are not trivial or self-centered. Millions of well-educated, talented, ambitious men and women are finding themselves dumped out in the cold, with little to salvage of their lost income and health benefits, prospects and hopes. Some are struggling to find their way back to the warmth of a safe employment environment, only to discover that such places are growing scarcer every day. The corporate middle management jobs that do remain are far more precarious than they were just a short time ago. Even those who maintain a hold on their jobs are feeling threatened and insecure. (See Figure 7-1.)

Disorientation and threat are a consequence of the very real shock of losing the familiar. Traditional forms of corporate communication—the memo moving up and down the hierarchy, the annual review, the company newsletter, the P&L statement—change in the organizational fishnet. People feel *out of touch* with one another and with the organization.

As the permanent workplace becomes a shifting work space, daily face-to-face contact with fellow workers is increasingly sporadic. The physical location of work is changing, even when a manager remains in a salaried position for a single employer. The office may truly be *any* place, and other employees in this new protean work environment will be expected to change sites and circumstances with great but unpredictable frequency.

This is partly the result of technological developments, of course, the same ones that contributed so resoundingly to the collapse of the Soviet Union and the communist regimes of Eastern Europe. The

- Organizational memory
- Control
- Work processes
- Conduit (up or down)
- Coordination
- "People stuff"
- "Work the system"

Figure 7-1 What middle managers used to do

speed of production has increased, and the distribution of workers and work flow has dispersed. The emerging breed of manager may have trouble understanding how these technologies can help, but without such an understanding they will be left behind.

It may be possible for workers in the new amorphous work space to stay in touch with the organization via electronic media, but the sense of connection is not the same as it was in the traditional workplace. Telecommuting gives a heady feeling of freedom at first, but it also can result in feelings of alienation, dissociation, feeling *out of place*. The anytime/anyplace business world leaves those whose position in the old hierarchy gave them status and power upset and uneasy. The fish-net rocks on the surface of a turbulent sea.

The traditional corporation had a "permanent" culture and conferred on employees a sense of belonging. A shared culture created a comfortable context. Moreover, a shared language and shared goals allowed the office team to function smoothly. When a newly hired manager joined a company, the first thing she learned was "the way things are done," the corporation's cast of characters and the connections between them, the history of the organization. When the manager received orders from above, each element arrived at a predictable time and belonged to an understood sequence. Continuity was not only critical; it was assumed.

It is no longer so dependable. The emerging "everywhere" office can interrupt employees at any time with requests and unexpected deadlines relayed via phone, fax, or e-mail. At the same time, companies are losing a sense of their own history, of continuity with the past and connection to the future. The result for individual employees can be a profound feeling of being *out of sync* with their organizations and co-workers, a feeling that can then extend to relations with their families, their friends, their communities, and themselves. If the office is everywhere, the individual is nowhere.

Meanwhile the diverse, global reach of fishnet organizations brings together individuals whose familiar patterns of working and interacting are no longer effective. Cosy, habitual routines are but a memory for most managers. The ten-fifteen coffee break, the hour lunch (let alone martini lunches), and the rush home at five o'clock sharp have all disappeared; work is time-driven, but it is no longer time-bound.

Corporations are redrawing their boundaries, trying to get more done with less. Increasing globalization of business makes cross-cultural skills mandatory, but few people have them. Native languages and all the "givens" of old cultures are dissolving. The rise of the new global economy means we must understand how people of other nations and cultures think about time and space, and more—much more. Much of how a person thinks is shaped by language. Concepts like *time* and *work* mean different things in different cultures and languages. Even within a single culture, this can be true across domains of expertise; marketers and engineers, for example, may use common terms to describe concepts that they nevertheless understand in significantly different ways. Despite the fact that English is almost universally used as the language of international business, speakers' native languages still color their attitudes and preconceptions in profound ways. The effect is that people feel *out of context*.

The emerging organizational territory has neither guidebooks nor guideposts to help employees acquire or regain a sense of balance with their environment. Managers have had to learn to read the subtle signals issued by corporate bureaucracies to determine the line between success and failure.

All the signals that were available in the past are gone, sweeping away painfully learned knowledge. When early hominids left the jungle and moved onto savannas, they had to give up ingrained understandings. Old familiar markers—the patterns of broken twigs, animal spoor—were replaced by new signs that were incomprehensible to the unpracticed eye. The awkward biped stood and looked out over the tops of the grass at a landscape empty of familiar landmarks. Information at a distance overwhelms, or creates mirages. That dark spot on the horizon coming rapidly closer might be a lion, but how could one be sure? It could just as easily be a friend.

The new environment—the technological and cultural territory we are moving into—forces us all to learn new skills, and learn them fast. The pace of such changes, and the learning required to handle them as they come along, will continue, and even increase. We must respond quickly, learning what we need to know to handle the immediate job, then be willing to let go and learn something else that is just as needed. Such just-in-time learning, or "performance support," can leave people feeling *out of balance*. It is too much change, too quickly.

Bill Bridges, a consultant who has written extensively about personal and organizational development, points out a consistent confusion between organizational change and transition.[1] *Change*, by his definition, is any radical shift in conditions, whether precipitated internally or externally: a stock market crash, the fall of the Berlin Wall, the peace agreement between Israelis and Palestinians in September 1993. It can happen very quickly, as is clear to anyone who has experienced a natural disaster. *Transition*, on the other hand, is the human process of getting used to change. The speed of transition is dictated by the time it takes people to develop new competencies, relationships, and flexibility under changed conditions. It is useful to consider whether those who are proposing quantum change through organizational re-design or reengineering are aware of this distinction. Laying off work-ers is a change; creating a new sense of work flow is a transition. Restructuring will lead to declining continuity in the short run, even if improved organizational balance eventually develops.

An implication of this distinction is that restructuring, redesign, and reengineering all involve both radical change and evolutionary tran-sition. The change might be implemented all at once, but transition strategies play out over longer periods and involve lots of practice and acceptance.

Reengineering doesn't just happen; it evolves. The metaphor is a mechanical one that is appropriate to organizational change but not to organizational transition. You don't just "do" reengineering; you *grow* it. To work, the metaphor must be mixed. A more organic metaphor is needed to describe the process of transition. It will not be simple, it will not be linear, and it will not be easy to implement. The transition to fishnet organizations requires time, something too few reengineered organizations have acknowledged.

AT&T is often used as an example of successful restructuring and reengineering, but it is also an example of the complexities of the tran-sition. For example, middle managers of AT&T used to provide a point of contact to (and for) the outside world. A single person at the middle management level with a project leadership role and a title like district manager would handle all dealings with important outside suppliers or contractors, purchasing resources and reselling or distributing them within the company. Sharing of resources across the corporation was encouraged and rewarded.

After the tens of thousands of layoffs and early retirements in the eighties and beyond, outside suppliers often no longer have that single point of contact within AT&T. Instead there are many contacts scat-tered throughout the company, and these employees have few incen-tives to cooperate with one another. For the contractor this means that the cost of sales goes up. For AT&T, it means little coordination across areas; outside consultants frequently tell one division of AT&T what other divisions are doing. Someone has to pay: AT&T's suppliers or contractors, AT&T itself, or AT&T's customers. Duplication of effort and lack of continuity are major problems since no one person or pro-cess is responsible for coordination.

AT&T's mixed success with its new organizational fishnet form raises the question of what middle managers used to do. Even if it turns out that some organizations might be better off with more middle managers, rather than fewer, there is no way to turn back the clock. The void left by the missing middle has workers and prospective workers wondering who's in charge.

Reengineering and reinvention leave fewer managerial spans and layers and less continuity. In today's slimmer organizations the middle managers who remain are stretched in ways they never could have imagined. Many are being spanned and layered beyond their ability to perform. They know that someone, or something, must take over the traditional functions that now go unfilled.

Among these key functions is organizational memory. Middle managers were once the repository of key content and business processes. Without them, the organization's constituents have nowhere to go to ask questions about how things should be done. Managers formerly controlled not only how and when things got done, but the more subtle and obscure details about who knew what, and when. Even if the mechanical details are preserved in reengineered corporations, the art is lost.

The best middle managers were very good at working the system, even when it involved skirting the rules and dodging official procedures. They were good jugglers, able to keep many balls in the air at the same time. They provided a conduit for information and ideas, passing them up and down hierarchies.

"Matrix" management notwithstanding, middle managers did not ordinarily communicate horizontally across different functions within the business unless they happened to carpool, play golf, or go bowling with people from other divisions. Yet this informal networking across division and department boundaries grew increasingly important and necessary as organizations grew both more rigid and more desperate to adapt to new market conditions. Downsizing often cut out coordinators, the people most important to these informal networks, leaving them in serious danger of collapse.

These managers were from the transitional period between the Organization Man age and the baby boomer generation. Like the Organization Men, they depended on their personal qualities to instill a cooperative and enthusiastic spirit in those they supervised. They were "people people" who coached and counseled younger managers. Elan Pitt is an example of a young executive who was helped by just such a mentor early in his career at a large manufacturer in Rochester, New

York. One windy winter day in 1993, Elan stumbled onto an early warning of times to come.

He had been uneasy for several months, though he hid it well. Only now did he realize what was wrong: he was going into a meeting without his boss, Mr. Fredericks.

Mr. Fredericks had been more than a boss; he was the personification of memory for their group, the man who knew how things worked, who knew the difference between what the company needed and what its employees needed, and maintained the balance. Elan trusted the older man. After all, Mr. Fredericks had gently taught him ever since he started three years before, and had given him greater responsibility as he became ready for it.

And then, suddenly, Fredericks was gone. He hadn't really wanted to leave, but the offer was good, and staying only created tension. He was just fifty-two, a year younger than Elan's father.

It was January, which probably meant he wouldn't get one last annual bonus, which his company was famous for. To Elan, Mr. Fredericks *was* the company, and because he had believed in him, Elan had believed in himself. Now he was on his own.

Elan's malaise outside the meeting room wouldn't go away. There were people on the other side of the door he didn't know. Would they take orders from him? Would they believe he could do the job? He pushed open the door. He had been right; he didn't know anyone in the room.

It had never been this way before. Elan had always worked with people he knew, people he had come to trust, on whom he could depend.

He must have paused a little too long, for the faces he saw around the table seemed to register skepticism, amusement, boredom—everything but the kind of welcoming support he was used to. Did they sense his weakness? Then he suddenly realized with a jolt that everyone in the room was thinking the same thing he was.

"Good morning," Elan said.

The nods around the table were not unfriendly, merely reserved, waiting.

"I know you've seen my résumé," he said, sitting down and opening his briefcase. "But let me fill in a little. I've been working with Mr. Fredericks for the past two years, both here and in Florida."

"We know all that," the balding man at the end of the table interrupted. Baskin, wasn't it? From finance? "But Mr. Fredericks is retiring Friday. The company is in trouble. We can't go along doing things the way we have been. We have to start over, and what you did with him doesn't matter. Not at all. This is a different team and a different project."

Elan bent his eyes to his briefcase as he took out his proposal. When he looked up again at the circle of eyes around the table, he knew that things had changed forever. He had to fly solo, and from now on every time would be the first time.

The survivors of reengineering, downsizing, rightsizing, and so on are asking themselves soul-searching questions about life after the lay-offs. Basic middle management functions still have to be done. But by whom—or what?

In fact, some middle management activities become *more* important after reengineering. Organizational memory and coordination take on a new importance for far-flung organizations powered by an outsource web of team members who barely know one another or the companies they are working for.

Managers in large corporations have traditionally fought to be at the center. In the fishnet organization, the center is the last place anyone wants to be. It is the dead zone, where innovation, excitement, and rewards are lacking. The action has moved to the edges.

8

Rewards, Loyalty, and Commitment

Corporations are increasingly stingy about offering comprehensive health and benefits packages. With co-payments increasing and benefits decreasing, individuals are forced to take more responsibility for their own skyrocketing health care costs and lost pension benefits while struggling to maintain their incomes.

The situation is growing precarious as more and more corporations are peopled by temporary employees. These companies would rather increase staff when the market requires it, but be free of commitments during slack periods. In fact, the concept of a temporary worker is changing. "Permanent temporaries" now have more career opportunities—not with the companies in whose buildings they actually work, but with the contracting companies, which develop long-term relationships with end employers. Call one of these permanent temporaries a "temp" at your own peril.

A growing army of contract workers is assembling in the distance, under the command of a new cadre of corporate generals, one or more steps removed from the actual jobs. Reengineering, restructuring, and the processes signified by the other *re*-words have reopened the social contract between employers and employees, although the terms of the new contract are still undefined.

Organizations are creating teams to marshal the resources of this diverse, sometimes motley workforce. Teams work well to increase the efficiency and timeliness of operations. The managers or paymasters in charge of teams, however, often have little sense of the motivations and incentives of the team members who work for them.

Leaders have no way of knowing just which team member is contributing what so they can establish a healthy set of incentives that in turn must remain in place over time. When processes are so complex nobody really understands them, employees feel like anonymous cogs in a big machine. Managers are left trying to give accurate performance reviews without guidelines.

In many companies, stated corporate values and policies do not filter down to the day-to-day actions of the firm. Systems to support work processes should provide direct embodiment of corporate values in a consistent manner, but in the post-reengineering universe they do not. There exists no preventive medicine for the pain of feeling excluded or underappreciated.

Whether in small service companies, such as those supplying software, telephone answering, investment planning, database processing, janitorial services, delivery, product development, or bookkeeping, or in complex global consultancies, inside or out, successful or struggling, no one yet understands what rewards will be meaningful in the new organizational environment. Neither companies that use entrepreneurial team members from outside the organization nor individual consultants who manage projects for client companies have managed to solve the problem of appropriate team rewards.

The question of rewards becomes even more difficult when team leadership is not clear. We hear one story being told over and over again, in many different ways, and with many different outcomes.

Dieter Rausch is the director of hardware development for a major U.S. manufacturer of computerized telephone systems for the international market. He got the news from a vice president one summer morning: just like the parent company, his company was required to downsize, and Dieter's department was not exempt. He needed to cut fourteen people from his division.

Dieter is a big, active engineer in his late forties. He skis in Europe, where he spends much of his time on business, and speaks English with a slight German accent. He is efficient and hardworking. He has an international orientation toward his job. He speaks three languages. Shrinking his department meant he would lose not engineers and designers but middle managers, the coordinators of disparate work activity across international lines and time zones as well as languages.

"Fourteen people!" Dieter exclaimed.

The vice president who had called him into his office for a little chat nodded.

Dieter was incredulous. "There won't be anyone left to do the managing. I've got more teams than that working already, with three more waiting to come on line."

"Not my problem," the vice president said with an airy wave of his hand. "We have every confidence in you. You'll figure it out."

Later, at a meeting of his department heads, Dieter raised the issue. The chart on the wall behind him showed the range of projects already under way, with a backlog of pending proposals. Removing the middle would be like removing the linchpin. He worried that the entire structure would collapse.

But there was no choice. He opened the meeting to suggestions.

"Why don't we try teams without managers?" Jennings, a wiry southerner, suggested. "Managers don't really do much anyway."

"Cutting people changes the ratio of money going out to money coming in," Dieter agreed. "But a team without a manager?"

"Worth a try, isn't it?" Jennings said.

Certainly it was worth a try. In fact, there were no other alternatives.

But after seven months the teams were adrift, and had accomplished little of substance. Dieter thought the problem was not so much that they had no managers. "The problem," he told his wife, "is that they have no leaders."

A team without a leader is a team with neither a cheering section and coach nor a scorekeeper. There is no one to judge who has contributed, whom to reward. Managers above the teams, like Dieter, can determine only what the entire team has accomplished, yet individuals still need to be acknowledged and encouraged.

The two perspectives, that of the manager and that of the team member, reveal disparate visions of these changes. The manager is concerned about how teams are orchestrated on various scales, with various combinations of players and various resources exchanged. Team members, on the other hand, are dominated by task and time concerns. There are few incentives to assist other teams unless such cross-working either helps both teams achieve immediate goals or is motivated by other, at present only vaguely defined, incentives, like company loyalty or obedience.

Lynda Applegate of the Harvard Business School interviews participants in Harvard's executive program and studies attempts to devise team reward systems for knowledge workers. So far, she is tracking companies that have put team reward systems in place across their corporate structures, though she has found only a few examples of white collar business units that have gone through a complete transition to self-managed teams and team rewards. In spite of flowery executive rhetoric promoting teams, most performance reviews still focus on individual performance.

In 1989, a nonprofit industry consortium, the Conference Board, featured an article on team reward systems in its magazine called *Across the Board*. It summed up the situation like this: "Teamwork sounds great, but my bonus depends upon meeting my numbers, and so does the other guy's."[1] Half a decade later, the situation has not improved much. Even though the problem is obvious, the solutions are not.

The lag in developing team incentives is a trap waiting to spring. Many of today's team members are running on the considerable excitement associated with being part of a successful team, but what will happen when the thrill is gone? It is already wearing thin for many people, even the high performers. Team members who are not rewarded fairly and in a way they can live with over time will crack, resist, or withdraw. Most corporations will wait for explosions before they recognize the problem and do something to respond. The flow of adrenaline is motivating, but it burns out quickly.

Senior executives are calling on employees to embrace the concept of business teams as a way to bypass organizational bureaucracy and see quick results. Can employees continue to be team players if they are rewarded only for individual performance? Competition among team members eats away the very underpinnings of successful teamwork.

In professional sports, superstars bring in the fans and fill the stadium seats, but this is not true of business superstars. Extreme gaps in compensation, while inevitable in professional sports today, can be fatal in business. The absence of team rewards is a major contributor to the declining sense of corporate loyalty many employees feel.

Mike Sollers, an independent contractor with an electronics firm, was edgy the afternoon we met. He had just heard news from the most recent round of reengineering at his corporation. Many of his friends, and two of his fellow team members, were on the early retirement list.

Mike knew he could be next. He also knew that, as an outside contractor rather than a full-time employee, he was less vulnerable than the permanent staff.

"It's strange," he says. "It's actually easier for me to be loyal to the company than it is for people who have worked here for ten years. It's the old-timers who are on the chopping block. They—or actually, their salaries and long-term benefits—look bad on the books; I don't."

Mike's wife works for a public utility company that provides family health insurance for its employees, and Mike is covered under his wife's policy. He hasn't thought much about retirement, though he is now forty-six years old. He has been a contractor at his current company for more than five years now, longer than he has ever worked for anyone. Mike is a software nomad.

"It's fun and it's fulfilling. We're building something, something good. My team is terrific. We have a great time and things really move. I've got more than enough to get by. I just hope it lasts."

For the past forty years the perquisites of employment with a large company among the Organization Man generation included security and regular opportunity for advancement. Work for a large company meant a lifelong career.

Beginning in the early eighties, the notion of job security began to seem quaint. A colleague from Sweden, long a stronghold of workers' rights, commented recently that what job security means nowadays is simply *having* a job. That such an observation was made by a Swede only underscores the reality of job insecurity in the United States and elsewhere.

Many Americans have traditionally defined themselves in terms of their jobs, but if workers are constantly changing positions and adopting new loyalties, self-concepts also change. Who are you—what is your identity when you don't have a job, don't have a career?

In general, many employers now prefer giving workers short-term ad hoc rewards rather than making long-term salary and benefit commitments. Alternatives to salary increases are already popular and likely to become more so. For example, the percentage of employees participating in defined contribution plans (such as stock ownership, profit sharing, and stock bonus plans) was 48 percent in 1989.[2] Such plans are attempts to build employee loyalty, even in the face of cutbacks in other benefits at a time of strong incentives to transfer these expenses to employees, or the consultants and vendors who have replaced them.

To fill the vacuum that appears every time a manager is laid off, new strains of middle management and middle managers are evolving. The shift away from a traditional full-time workforce means the terms of work are under renegotiation. The effect of fewer long-term employees and lower corporate commitment to provide job security and benefits like health care results in employees who are less inclined to be loyal toward employers. "What's in it for me?" they ask.

A headline from Silicon Valley's *San Jose Mercury News* on September 21, 1992, reads SELF-EMPLOYED SPECIALISTS TO FILL AMERICAN WORK FORCE OF THE FUTURE. Similar headlines are appearing around the country. Articles like this remind workers that long-term employment with a single company is a thing of the past. People who might in another generation have been interested in planning their careers are now obsessed with just getting a job, or holding on to the one they have.

The disenchantment affects all workers, even before they are ever laid off. Dan Reynolds, a self-confident engineer with twenty years' experience with large companies, was laid off in 1992. Once Dan had had a good career ahead of him with a manufacturer of telephone switching equipment. When his company was bought out, it became a subsidiary of one of the largest corporations in the world, a powerful and dominant presence in the computer industry. By the late eighties Dan was a middle manager working for a new group investigating the potential of the emerging complex of technologies called "multimedia."

"My boss hired two consultants to prepare a report. They were friends of his, real estate developers with no expertise whatsoever in media, much less multimedia. It was a fiasco. I called some of my friends and asked them, informally, to try to bring the two consultants up to speed. A year later I was laid off."

Caught in frenzied downsizing, Dan joined the legions of independent consultants. His tombstone might read DAN REYNOLDS WAS EXCESSED AS PART OF HIS COMPANY'S RIGHTSIZING.

"But my God—the company had become completely dysfunctional," he says. "There was no incentive to produce. Initiative was punished. New groups were forming and dissolving every day, with new, fuzzy missions and incomplete support. *Upper* management didn't have any idea whether they would be there in a week or a month, much less middle management. It was impossible to feel loyalty to the constantly changing environment. When my boss gave a sixty-thousand-dollar contract to his friends, I knew the end was coming. How could I feel any loyalty to an organization that allowed stuff like that? The company was imploding, and it was a relief to leave."

Not much loyalty there. Not much loyalty in many places where loyalty used to exist. During a recent visit to the headquarters of an international company, we talked with a leading technology planner who had worked on many global teams in recent years. Knowing of our interest in business teams, he blurted out, with considerable frustration, "Teams are dead!"

He argued that global companies have become so diffuse, with so few shared values and so little corporate loyalty, that it is no longer reasonable to assume employees are willing to build teams—to become familiar with one another's work style, develop trusting relationships, clarify goals, and so on. Team building takes too long and there are too few incentives for people to do the work it requires.

The senior manager observed that team leaders are becoming more like pushers than facilitators, bargaining and trading in order to get enough of whatever they need to move ahead. Managers may think that a team is doing the work, but it is certainly not a team in any cohesive sense. The so-called team is nothing but a loosely structured aggregation of employees trying to survive in the changed business environment.

Dieter Rausch would agree. He had no idea how to turn his leaderless teams into alliances for action; he just hoped things would work out. But they were not working out for Dieter, and they are not working out for many corporations and employees.

The idea of business teams, of course, is not really dead. Under the right circumstances teams can be very effective. Company loyalty is in question, however, and assuming workers' commitment to their corporations is unwarranted. Without commitment, teams become opportunistic and divisive. Team members work well together only when self-serving motivations are in alignment.

As yet there are only crude corporate team reward systems. And without a widespread and comprehensive system of team rewards, corporate loyalty and commitment will continue to rot away.

9
Media
Mismatch

Dennis left the sales department of his large industrial corporation for a small start-up. When he arrived at the new company he made a point of going to everyone's office and introducing himself. "Hi," he would say gustily, charging through the door with his hand extended. "I'm Dennis. I'm here to help you all get up and running, move the units."

He was greeted with ambivalent enthusiasm. When the vice president asked people how they liked the new sales director, they shrugged. "He seems nice," they said. "A little pushy, but I guess that's OK if he pushes the product."

It wasn't until he started leaving messages on his colleagues' voice mail or interrupting through the office intercom that the trouble began. "Dennis here," he would boom over the speaker phone. "My office, ten minutes. Urgent." Then he'd hang up.

The first time he issued Elaine this kind of peremptory summons, she looked at the phone as if it had just delivered an uninvited touch. She was seething. She stormed over to Sally's office. "He left me a message," she fumed.

Sally looked up. "Dennis?"

Elaine had at first been surprised by Dennis's message, but only for a moment. "He's bossy," she said. "Rude. Sexist. Pushy."

"Obnoxious," Sally agreed.

"'My office. Ten minutes,'" Elaine mimicked. "Screw him. I've got work to do."

"Well," Sally said, smiling, "which is more important?"

Elaine smiled too. "I'm not even in sales. All he wants is to ask me to spell out the features of the new product. Everything that's already in the sales manual. He doesn't bother to read the stuff—he just wants people to hold his hand, telling him what he needs to know."

"Maybe he's used to face-to-face meetings, contact with other people, getting it from the—"

"Horse's mouth." Elaine laughed out loud. "OK, I'll do it one more time. But this is it, I promise."

Style is modified by medium. With most people Dennis's expansiveness is effective when he meets with them in person, yet he can come across as obnoxious through the web of interconnecting electronic media. An attitude construed as enthusiasm when conveyed face to face is indistinguishable from aggression in voice-mail messages or faxes. A person who writes concise e-mail messages may seem impulsive, opportunistic, pushy, overbearing, foolish, or simply rude.

Electronic media, filtering tone of voice and body language out of messages, also hinder feedback regarding how recipients are reacting. Delivery must be tempered to match the medium, but guidelines for using the new media are evolving (as such rules do) in an ad hoc, informal, uncontrolled way.

Corporations are no help, either. Current training manuals give little advice regarding how hard to push, how often to leave messages, or what the thresholds of bad behavior in a virtual electronic universe might be. Even courses in effective communication rarely include instruction on media use.

When different kinds of people are thrown together in temporary teams, behavioral protocols are even more significant, and at the same time more difficult to discern. The fishnet organization calls for changing roles, attitudes, expectations, and cultures at a moment's notice.

Without attention to these issues, the result is confusion. In "Marooned in a Blizzard of Lies," the jazz musician Dave Frishberg laments,

> We must have lunch real soon
> Your luggage is checked through
> We've got inflation licked
> I'll get right back to you
>
> It's just a standard form
> Tomorrow without fail
> Pleased to meet you, thanks a lot
> Your check is in the mail

We'll send someone right out
Now this won't hurt a bit
He's in a meeting now
The coat's a perfect fit

Strictly fresh today
Service with a smile
I'll love you darling till I die
We'll keep your name on file

We easily recognize the clichés of the contemporary business culture, overused for satire. Problems arise when we expect the words we hear to mean what we think they mean. In organizations that are constantly in flux, however, they rarely do.

When corporations add the visual medium of video teleconferencing (coming soon to a desktop near you), the behavioral changes demanded by the medium are subtle and troubling. Video may *seem* like the next best thing to being there, but electronically mediated interactions are different from real-life meetings. A video image is both less real than real life, because it is television, and more real, because the real-life happenings we usually watch on television are called news. This affects our attitudes and beliefs about what we see and hear. Each medium has its own hidden bias, and we are just beginning to understand what these biases are.

Companies tend to assume that, despite its expense, video capability would be a great aid to them in the way they do business. In the early seventies, however, an intriguing set of experiments done at the Communications Studies Group at University College in London raised questions about the limits of this assumption. In the study, researchers compared the ability to detect lying in face-to-face encounters, through video teleconferencing, and through audio alone. The subjects of the experiments were paired off, and one subject was asked to tell a lie to the second through various media. The second subject then had to figure out whether the first was lying or not. The researchers concluded that it was easier to detect lying over audio only than it was through either video or face-to-face contact.[1]

Our current assumptions regarding which electronic media will be most valuable in what situations are likely to be off base and even misleading. After all, they are founded on previous experience. We are unaware that when we think of new media (video conferencing, for example), we do so in terms of old ones (face-to-face meetings). We have created a metaphor, and we think that because the two things are similar and serve the same function, they *are* the same. They are not the same; they are only similar. We are misled by that similarity into thinking there is no difference.

It is doubtful that face-to-face meetings are the ideal form of group communication in all situations. It is equally doubtful that more media richness is always better.

Video teleconferencing may offer more media diversity than we need, and it can be misused easily. People who are good at deception are usually very good at using visual cues as a distraction. As yet our instincts about which electronic medium will be best for which purposes are not to be trusted. We will have to learn how to use a variety of media, across a wide range of situations, and with a mix of people.

Teleconferencing is only one of the new media. As the multitudes of former middle managers spill into the new world of business in the twenty-first century, they will find themselves spending more and more time driving to work not on a concrete highway, but on an information superhighway that isn't like any highway they have ever experienced—a highway that is no highway at all. The anytime/anyplace office is highly mobile and dependent on computer systems, which still have steep learning curves and are prone to failure, as well as too-rapid innovation and obsolescence.

Managers like Dennis are forced to use new methods, forced in have their personalities and social style mediated by networks, voice mail, video. If they cannot learn to adapt, they will suffer the consequences. In the short term, media mismatches will occur over and over again. Gradually, people will learn which media are good for what. Then sharing this learning across teams of teams will become a problem of organizational memory. Communications technology can help in the creation of fishnet organizations, but it cannot heal the gaping wounds left by the rupture of the old corporate monolith.

No one predicted the rise of desktop publishing, or the fax machine, or CNN, or the VCR. Nobody yet knows, and no one will know for at least a decade, which communications media are suitable for which business purposes. Under such circumstances, all our assumptions about the use of the new media in business will most certainly be wrong, or at best, misguided.

10

Boundaries, Borders, and Frontiers

Like the Berlin Wall in 1989, more and more traditionally monolithic dividers have shattered, crumbled, or faded away. The European Union, for example, now allows citizens of its member countries to travel across national borders without passports. Even though new barriers have emerged in the world with bewildering velocity in regions like the former Yugoslavia and Soviet Union, many others are evaporating.

Boundaries, borders, and frontiers are subtly different from one another, yet they are the stuff of which environments are made. Boundaries are most rigid, their outline obvious and often oppressive. At the other extreme, frontiers can be frightening in their very flexibility.

As the work environment changes and the shape of business organizations warps beyond recognition, the definition of edges and limits also blurs and shifts. How we think about such divisions results from our attitudes, our culture, and the metaphors we use to describe them.

A boundary is an edge or limit; a boundary contains. One can go up to the boundary, but no farther. It is a wall, a fence, a marker to identify extent. There is no real other side to a boundary. Others may exist out there on the other side, of course, but they are not important because they do not give us identity. A boundary like the speed of light, absolute zero, or the size of the universe has only one side—our own.

Traditional boundaries between and within corporations are going the way of the Berlin Wall. Onetime business divisions in which middle managers played the role of vertical expediters are disappearing. Managers are finding ways to work across formerly rigid boundaries, to exceed their limits, to move the boundaries out of the way or get rid of them altogether.

Many of the boundaries, borders, and frontiers of the new fishnet organization do not even appear on company charts. The middle managers who pioneered this territory were often the first to fall victim to downsizing, and the organization areas that remain are described by old-style upper managers whose metaphors belong to an earlier age.

It was the middle managers who used to forge many of the personal connections within organizations: horizontal alliances and cross-divisional relationships that increased work efficiency. These managers now carry their Rolodexes with them into the spaces between organizations. On an organizational level, transcorporate strategic alliances and ad hoc working teams have emerged, sometimes producing and sometimes not, then disappeared again. Every time a cross- corporate team succeeds, the limits that boundaries imply break down further.

Boundary loss is signaled by the sculptured corporate logos decorating the sloping green lawns of America's industrial enclaves. New shapes sprout and metamorphose before our eyes. The initials of businesses speed through an alphabet soup at mind-numbing speed. Harper and Row, the publishing company that in the sixties publicly swore it would never buy out or be bought, became the morphed and merged HarperCollins by the early nineties. What was once an industry populated by entities with well-defined boundaries, staffed by well-read editors in tweed coats, has become a small set of conglomerates run by pinstriped MBAs focused not on letters but on numbers—the bottom line, a fact reflected on the title pages of recent books. Some boundaries remain within the conglomerates, but they are rapidly disintegrating.

So it is that boundaries disappear. Borders, too, are under attack. A border is a dividing line marking an abrupt shift between two separate, sometimes antagonistic, entities. It is a narrow transition zone, apt to change with the political winds. A customs agent demands our passports; a corporate security guard hands us visitor's passes at a rival corporation's reception area. When we cross a border, we know we have moved from one psychological space to another. In the early nineties, Apple and IBM created an alliance called Taligent, and buildings with the Taligent logo in front of them have cropped up throughout the Apple corporate campus.

Even that looming temporal border, the watershed between the twentieth and the twenty-first centuries, now so close, seems to wobble as the debate over whether the new century starts in 2000 or 2001 heats up. Time dissolves before us: growing seasons and the cycles of day and night are irrelevant to the increasing sophistication of the worldwide communications net, along with the insistent clamor of cellular telephones, faxes, and audio or video conferencing. The position of the sun makes no difference to the sleepless flow of global business.

Frontiers, the indefinite open spaces at the farthest edges, are beyond the borders and boundaries of known territory. On the frontier, laws are flexible—if they exist at all. Some nations think of the space beyond their own borders as frontier; in imagination it is lawless simply because it is Other. In these countries the idea of boundaries or rigidly defined limits, may be mingled with that of borders, making both into a frontier.

The historical American ideal of the frontier was of a place that offered limitless opportunity to those with courage and initiative, despite what some perceived as a desolate and empty landscape. It was a destination for people on the move. They could stay one step ahead of persecution or the law, could escape the restricted options more settled areas presented, and find room to breathe. The frontier was a place where laws were uncertain or difficult to enforce.

Yet it was also a turbulent place, filled with hostile challenges: blizzards, wild animals, renegades, natives. To the settler or trapper or cattleman, the western frontier was both promising and dangerous. And of course, to the native peoples, the very same place was not a frontier at all; it was home.

Frontiers constantly move out ahead of us, followed by the safe, the settled, the known. To the human resources manager in today's organizations, new forms of work and new ways of organizing time represent a frontier, a limitless, borderless, boundaryless unknown where anything can happen, and often does. To the teleworker, entrepreneur, or team manager, that same territory is coming to be home.

How sharply will corporate organizations manage to define themselves as the information era unfolds? Boundaries and borders will lose clarity and definition. A country is defined largely by its citizens, who share a common notion of who they are and common loyalty to national ideals. Corporations have turned fluid. Their edges run, fade, move. Their citizens are restless and rootless, moving from company to company with ease, taking with them a little of each culture when they leave.

Are corporations prepared to deal with this reversion of formerly settled territory to frontier? Probably not.

Mergers, acquisitions, joint ventures, and megacorporations, not to mention cross-company teams, often result in strange bedfellows. Information systems simultaneously simplify and complicate the problem. A corporation's electronic tentacles can stretch around the world, where they tangle with the reach of other corporations. The very definition of a corporation is called into question on a daily basis.

The idea of redrawing corporate lines as required by shifts in the business world is attractive. Such a redrawing would allow an organization to be reconfigured for specific projects, but not permanently commit the funds and resources to maintain these capabilities beyond immediate needs. At the same time, the overlapping of boundaries raises questions about corporate security, and legal questions about who owns what.

For those working at the shifting borders of business, the psychological strain is even greater. In an article in the *Harvard Business Review*, Larry Hirschhorn and Thomas Gilmore define four psychological boundaries that are under siege in the emerging global business environment: the authority boundary (Who is in charge of what?), the task boundary (Who does what?), the political boundary (What's in it for us?), and the identity boundary (Who is—and isn't—one of us?).[1] The authors imply skepticism about the seeming absence of boundaries in the new organizational climate; they conclude that boundaries remain, though they have changed their position and their nature.

These dimensions apply equally to employees of new fishnet organizations and to team members working outside traditionally defined business spaces. Because boundaries between employees' traditional roles in the work environment are disappearing, pressure to recognize and acknowledge the roles themselves is increasing.

Although often oversimplified or oversold, some of the principles of the human potential movement bear on business organizations. Self-awareness of roles and of the feelings evoked in interpersonal encounters is increasingly critical for the nimble entrepreneur. The web of relationships forms the substrate for future business as boundaries move into psychological space and lose their physical definition.

Remember George Radcliffe, the vice president for a clothing manufacturer who constantly has to remind himself that a cubicle in the middle of the building is a reaffirmation of his central leadership role? He is an example of someone who has become lost or disoriented on the new frontier. His new boundaries are psychological and electronic, and even after six months of reengineering, he remains bewildered about where the limits are and what they mean.

For George, only one of the traditional boundaries is intact: his identity is still closely tied to his corporation, as it has been for his entire adult working life. The authority and task boundaries that define his position, however, continually shift like sand. He is sometimes group leader, sometimes attentive listener, sometimes problem solver. The political boundary is also in flux: at times he holds the point of view of his team, working to bring the ordering and sales process closer to the customer, and at times he must distance himself to embrace the views of affiliated teams.

When George's borders and boundaries went, they took with them his understanding of who and where he was. "I get home late at night," he says, "and I'm exhausted. And it's not a good kind of tired."

Business teams cross traditional division, professional, and corporate lines. If a team needs a piece of information or a type of expertise, it is very likely to go for it directly and not puzzle about protocols. With the cultural shift to business teams, traditional organizational boundaries become secondary and are often ignored, leaving companies open to unresolved security issues. The "worm" that invaded the Internet in the fall of 1988 and grabbed the attention of the national press had a major effect on the perceptions of many nontechnical managers.[2] The actual violation was not new, but the coverage was extraordinary. What used to be a subject of interest only to computer nerds was on the front page of every business paper.

The response of executives to concerns about security, however, has been uneven and often naive. Many managers tend to view computer security and computer crime as technological problems that technicians can solve. In fact, security issues go far beyond what is technologically controllable. Corporate security is not 100 percent effective, at any price. In a world of shifting boundaries, vanishing borders, and proliferating frontiers, security is even more difficult to achieve. Technical fixes cannot assure it. Violations are a gnawing reminder that corporate walls are growing ever thinner. As employees carry (or wear) increasingly powerful computers with them, security becomes a matter of personal habits and practices more than technical control. Each traveling employee becomes an independent security agent. Everyone is an amateur in this world, except the growing proportion of electronic criminals.

Some companies have tried to control their electronic boundaries with virtual guard dogs and armed sentries. Not only does this approach not work, but there can be severe backlash. Overcontrol smothers the creativity of individual expression and exchange across corporate and global lines. What Mitch Kapor and John Perry Barlow call the electronic frontier is not yet governed by laws that would protect the security of global organizations, nor does the capability to enforce such laws exist.[3] At a recent major workshop with corporate and university sponsorship, the leader of a large international company that works across borders was asked about legal requirements in global settings. He replied that "international law is unenforceable." The electronic frontier requires its pioneers to be resourceful in defending themselves in the absence of binding rules and regulations.

In the new business environment, if you can't tell the difference among boundaries, borders, and frontiers, you're in trouble, both in terms of the problems you will face and the opportunities you will miss. And at this time, most organizations cannot tell the difference.

11

Love and
(Over)Work

Psychologists since Freud have speculated that we can track the true meaning of dreams to either love or work and interpret them in the light of one or both. Balancing the two has always been difficult, but it will be even more delicate in the next century as more people move out of the comfortable womb of corporate office life. The boundary between office and home is thinning to transparency in the information era. Telecommuting, at-home work, entrepreneurial teams, and the ad hoc alliances forming among consultants working with the leaner global businesses of the future all contribute to new kinds of stress—and new opportunities—at the intersection of love and work.

An executive with a *Fortune* 100 company recently sent us an article from the *Wall Street Journal* on the growing pressures of working globally via electronic media. Accompanying the article was a scrawled note: "I'm already finding that voice mail and portable computers are creating an expectation that everyone is on call all the time." This experienced global worker was rudely alerted to an early warning: the anytime/anyplace office, once a vision of hope for many overworked managers of the eighties, can turn into the all-the time/every place office, a vision of hell rapidly taking form in the real world. Workers must learn to balance the often conflicting demands of love and work amid the commonplaces of flextime, job sharing, and simple telecommuting.

Clean air is a major problem in such metropolitan areas as Los Angeles, Phoenix, Denver, New York, and Washington. These areas are becoming increasingly aggressive in limiting automobile use to preserve air quality. Most of these efforts are currently voluntary. But air quality is a deep concern that is only beginning to surface. It is clear that something has to be done. Mandatory requirements are here already in some regions and forthcoming in others, and companies will have to play their part in contributing to decreased automobile commuting. Telecommuting is no longer a vague vision, but a requirement, displacing all the physical and mental points of reference to which we have become accustomed. Such points of reference are, of course, shaped by culture.

Events to date represent only the beginnings of a more profound shift. The transition to anytime/anyplace work is not likely to be a graceful one. In the short run, a pattern of overwork at home is most likely. It is all too easy to fall into a pattern of chain-working—lighting the next task from the embers of the first—to the detriment of love and family, the needs of children or aging parents.

The new worker, already besieged by constant change, is subject to a relentless fear and uncertainty about health care and retirement security (not to mention whether the next contract will materialize). Now, as an often self-employed entrepreneur, the newly flexible worker finds that travel schedules, international conference calls, middle-of-the-night faxes, and round-the-clock messages on e-mail intrude on all aspects of life, smearing over twenty-four hours, weekends, and holidays. (See Figure 11-1.)

The erosion of the comfortable routine of the workday, at a designated workplace, with evenings and weekends off for rest and relaxation is reflected in the lifestyle of former Apple Computer chairman John Sculley, who commented recently that the notion of sleeping eight straight hours through the night is an "obsolete remnant of the agrarian and industrial eras."[1]

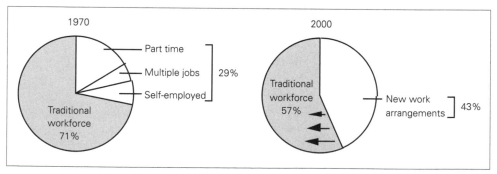

Figure 11-1 Growth of the flexible workforce

Sculley himself typically wakes at three-thirty each morning to catch business news from Japan and Europe; he rarely sleeps for eight hours at a stretch. He naps and works, naps and works. Mostly he works, like other frenzied executives who are chasing the elusive global workday. Along with an increasing number of managers far below his stature, role, and level of compensation, he works anywhere and everywhere. For many, the anytime office has already become the all-the-time office.

Soon, you will be on an airplane flight and the phone in front of your seat will ring. The call will be for you, from a caller who knows you better than do many of your co-workers. But the caller won't be a good friend; she'll be a telemarketer who knows not only your lifestyle preferences and your spending habits but your flight time and seat number, as well as who is sitting next to you and how many miles each of you has in frequent flyer accounts. The caller will have made a pretty accurate estimate of how many drinks you had before the call and what stage you are at in your meal service on the flight; her timing is impeccable. You may cringe as you read this, and perhaps at the time you receive the first such call, you will experience a sense of violation. Something will have changed, become utterly different in a way that will gnaw at you, while it simultaneously intrigues you. And in your airplane seat sometime in the not-distant future you may also experience a sense of relief because the telemarketer has given you the opportunity to buy something you want and need at the time you need it, with no extra effort.

When it is enacted, this scenario will verify that interlinked databases have targeted you as a good candidate for a particular product. An intelligent computer-based agent will have determined that you will be on that flight at that time, in that seat. Almost universal access has become possible, even when the person being contacted does not want it to occur.

Round-the-clock access can mean that workers have no time of complete rest or release. The same electronic system that provides flexibility to care for children or elderly parents at home can function as an electronic leash.

Overwork at home has its advantages from the corporate point of view: it means extra work for no extra pay. What corporation would argue with that? But from an employee's or contractor's point of view, and even from the long-term point of view of the corporation, the most obvious pitfall is overworking, with deleterious health effects and eventually lower performance.

Overworking will be magnified by health issues surrounding computer use. Companies are just beginning to recognize these issues in the office, which after all is a much more controlled setting than the home or the road. In the race for portability, ergonomics takes a back seat to size and convenience. Health effects are likely to lurk in the basement or the hall closet, which has been converted into an office cubicle for the ill-prepared teleworker.

This office with a view to anywhere promises new options for flexible work, and new freedom for workers themselves to determine when and where they do it, but it may not deliver in the way we want it to. Many jobs, for instance, require workers in effect to be in two or more places at once. The worker must straddle and stretch across the distances, often very large distances.

More subtle pressures relating to meetings are already assumed to be inevitable. Managers spend anywhere from 30 to 70 percent of their time communicating with others, typically in two-person meetings, although they also spend massive blocks of time cloistered in conference rooms. Business travel is a partial solution to meet some communications needs, but today's global business communications needs are just too great to be satisfied by physical travel alone. Travel is desirable, and even enjoyable, up to a threshold amount, but many workers have been flown far beyond that amount. Although common today, travel frenzies are rarely productive, particularly for global managers. Meanwhile the need to communicate, or at least coordinate, is accelerating. Add to this the fact that managers now working with a company rather than within it are often responsible for their own travel expenses, and the pressure increases.

The new post-reengineering, entrepreneurial managers for hire are on call all the time, everywhere: under the banner "Have skills will travel," "Will middle-manage for food." As a consequence, little or no time is left for the responsibilities and rights of community and family.

Rites are affected as well. As Max DePree suggests in *Leadership Is an Art,* one of the warning signs of institutional deterioration and increasing entropy is that organizations no longer make time for ritual and ceremony, two important human activities tied to love but all too often expressed, in modern society, through work.[2] Company picnics, Halloween parties, and award banquets are important.

It is not uncommon for people who meet on computer networks to fall in love without ever seeing one another in person.[3] They may well have lovers or spouses in real life (what network surfers call IRL).

What if love happens at work, and the lovers have other lovers at home?

Amy and Sean, for instance, were members of a global team designing a delivery system for an important multinational customer. Sean's life had always been well organized—some might have said too much so. His accounting practice had grown, and he was invited to participate in a new business team, where he met Amy, a talented marketing manager with a diverse client base. Both had families.

They exchanged e-mail messages that started off being strictly business, but that began to include personal notes, reflections on the local weather (he was in Seattle, she in Vancouver). At the first of a long series of monthly face-to-face meetings of the entire team, they spent more time together than business warranted.

The team was under extreme time pressure. Amy and Sean's work was essential to the project, and their contribution was enormously appreciated by the other members of the team, but their relationship was growing too intense for the team's comfort. At the monthly meetings they took their meals together and did not appear to welcome anyone else to join them. At first the others joked about it, but their air of exclusivity began to affect team performance. When a second deadline slipped, Sarah, the team leader, decided to talk to them about it privately.

They were indignant. How could she think such a thing? They both had families! Their homes were sacrosanct; they would never jeopardize family for a work relationship.

Sarah pointed out the meals they took together, how they often retreated to a private corner of the hotel lounge to talk, the number of times they disappeared together. Even if there was nothing to it, their behavior was damaging the project. Such pairing off on business teams was not unusual, but people were talking. Maybe it was the missed deadline that raised the issue; it made everyone irritable.

Amy and Sean agreed to pay more attention to their work and to how they were perceived by others on the team. They spent less time together, and more time interacting with the rest of the team. The quality of work improved.

A year later, though, Sean got a divorce. Amy remained undecided for another two years before she left her relationship. And all that time there had been nothing between them—that is, nothing physical. "It's just that working with Sean was so *real*," Amy said later, with a rueful laugh. "I always thought Bill was my 'significant other,' but I never felt that way with him. Maybe it was the project, the time pressure. Maybe it just was some kind of chemistry between me and Sean; I don't know. I don't see Sean anymore, but I just couldn't stay with Bill."

Confusion between love and work is one danger posed by the collapse of the wall between the two. It is also a side effect of the intensity and excitement of work teams.

Organizations like the Families and Work Institute and the Conference Board, a nonprofit consortium supported by some of the world's largest corporations, have begun an exchange on work-family issues and the work ethic. One member of the Conference Board asked at a meeting in 1993 why it was that businesses so often equated hours of work with productivity, and measured only the hours.

One answer, of course, is that it is easy to measure hours and difficult to measure productivity. But measuring only time is also, as many have noticed, spurious; time spent on a project is often unrelated to actual productivity. Watching television or playing ball with a child may not seem to be work, but if the activity triggers an idea or results in a sudden insight, then television viewing or playing ball *is* work, as well as time with family. But because there are no effective ways to quantify these moments or predict when they will occur, guilt may drive the worker back to the home office. Such clock-punching may in fact be counterproductive.

Telework from home will become more and more common, but not as common as overwork at home. Many managers will not commute every day to an office in the morning and leave in the afternoon the way the middle managers of the past used to.

It is ironic that the pain of too much work or too little time to do it is exacerbated by the introduction of the very technology that was supposed to solve problems of time and place in the short term. A busy executive with too much to do may bring home a laptop computer or install a home fax machine only to find that he now does more work out of office hours than he did before. Technology is not an easy fix. More than a mere media mismatch, the invasion of home life is an indication that the window to anywhere will not solve communications problems. Technology creates the potential for solutions, but even the best communications systems will not make people communicate if they do not want to or do not know how.

In the early seventies, teleconferencing links were just being brought into rural Canada, connecting villages across wide expanses of the continent. Before the advent of telecommunications, some of these villages had no major roads and few links to the outside world beyond bush airplanes.

An old man was asked, "Isn't it wonderful that all these isolated villages are now connected with each other, and with the major cities?"

"Depends what they talk about," he answered.

The same is true now: information technologies create the potential for new types of organizations and new variations in the love-and-work formula. To date, however, little thought has been given to balancing love and work through creative use of communications media.

We have not found a single U.S. corporation that has a sophisticated policy for encouraging such a balance between personal life and work. There is great potential for creative work arrangements, but right now the potential for pain is greater.

Since no company has a policy to guard against overwork by home workers, the implicit policy is that such workers are expected to overwork. An anonymous executive bluntly stated the Silicon Valley standard, "We keep them until they burn out, and then we replace them." Such a condition cannot endure. Soon enough the legions of teleworkers will rebel and set their own policies.

12

The Widening Gap

When even successful and secure workers are feeling the stress of balancing the demands of love and work, how much worse can it be for those relegated to the fringes of economic well-being? On the dark side of diversity is this ugly problem: much of the world's population is already so deep in an economic and social quagmire that it is unlikely they will surface within their lifetimes. It is not just a one-generation problem; it has been going on for a long time, with no break in sight. An information underclass has emerged, dominated by diverse people cut off from the organizational transformations of the information age. About 25 percent of U.S. households are stuck in poverty, and the proportion of households in the United States with income levels below $15,000 a year (in 1991 dollars) has remained constant over the last two decades. These figures are unlikely to change.

The middle class, as measured by the percentage of households at each income level, is fading. By the year 2000, Institute for the Future forecasts suggest that only about 30 percent of U.S. households will be categorized as middle class. Since the absolute number of households in the United States has grown during the past two decades, the actual numbers of households stuck in poverty also grew almost 40 percent to around thirty-five million Americans, many of them children.[1]

During this same period, the number of people with year-round full-time jobs who are of low-income status leaped by almost 50 percent.[2] The message: first, a full-time job no longer offers access to the middle class; second, many middle-class jobs are no longer full-time. A shifting constellation of part-time jobs is becoming the middle-class norm.

Job seekers who lack the education to use information resources effectively are at a disadvantage. In flexible organizations, computer and information-related skills are vital. Today such skills are directly correlated with socioeconomic class. For instance, nearly every household has a television set, but relatively few have personal computers. A recent survey conducted by the Institute for the Future with Louis Harris and Associates found that 11 percent of all U.S. households are "infomated," meaning that they are heavy users of information technology. (In the survey, *infomated* was defined as having any five of eight key information technologies in the household: answering machine, cellular phone, CD music player, fax machine, laser disc player, personal computer, VCR, and voice mail service.) Home ownership of personal computers is especially important because it correlates with higher computer test scores later in life and an increased probability of working with computers in secondary and postsecondary education programs.[3]

The situation is even worse for single-parent households. And minorities, African Americans in particular, are least likely to have information technology skills. In 1989, less than 50 percent of blacks and only about 40 percent of Hispanics had used computers, as opposed to nearly 60 percent of non-Hispanic whites and 70 percent of Asians. The gap has widened since then.[4]

Thus an increasing proportion of the next generation of workers will enter the job market without the skills they need. From a company's point of view, newly hired employees not needing significant training will be increasingly scarce. The current political climate in Washington does not suggest that government programs can be relied on to fill this training gap.

Central government monitoring of equality for minorities is giving way to team-driven job markets with simultaneously increasing and decreasing opportunities for minorities: immediate opportunities for anyone with the training for them, but nothing for those without the right education. Those who fail to gain the skills they need will find themselves the victims of an invisible form of discrimination, with no opportunity for redress.

The good news is that anyone who possesses information and learning skills is likely to find a job, old-boy networks notwithstanding. For those with the preparation, traditional barriers like the glass ceiling will weaken or disappear completely. For those without such preparation, however, the picture is much more bleak.

The United States has traditionally offered the poor relatively easy access to the middle class if they can find steady work. But the number of steady jobs has dwindled, and it is unlikely that time by itself will improve the picture. Even for those who are most fully qualified, full-time jobs with full-time benefits are scarce.

This shift away from job stability is reflected in the increased numbers of sales workers in the retailing industry (up 44 percent during the eighties) and of service workers, many of whom are part time and semiskilled (up 14 percent). At the end of the eighties there were 30 percent fewer managers for this dispersed, high-turnover workforce made up of people who often have little corporate loyalty, for good reason. The need for continuity in industries like this is daunting: fewer people must manage more workers. Such a formula simply cannot work for employer or employee.

Meanwhile the population is changing in fundamental ways. Overall population growth has slowed markedly, and the huge baby-boom group is now middle-aged. Younger age groups are experiencing a rapid increase in the proportion of minorities among their ranks. Black, Hispanic, and other minorities currently constitute 22 percent of the U.S. population. By the year 2000, this share will have grown to 26 percent overall; among Americans thirty years of age or younger, minorities will make up 30 percent or more of the population. In California they will make up more than 50 percent. The minority population is growing faster than its white counterpart because it is typically younger, has higher fertility rates, and in recent years has gained the most people via immigration.

The proportion of minorities is increasing just as the rules of the game are changing, but the difference in opportunity runs deeper than access to computer skills. The gap between "have" and "have not" children is widening. In 1992, more than 22 percent of children under eighteen lived in poverty.[5] At the other extreme, approximately 27 percent of children lived in households earning more than $50,000 a year.

As the workforce grows more diverse ethnically, the average worker's age will rise from thirty-five to forty by the year 2000. These older workers, who expect promotions and increasing compensation, health and family benefits in exchange for performance, are facing the loss of all of these. Large global organizations are unable to keep their promises to provide these benefits. This older, more diverse workforce will pose difficult organizational problems.

In one of its "Second Century" features, the *Wall Street Journal* has described this situation as a "demographic imperative" that will force corporations to become more active in training future workers. It argues that the workforce shortages and workforce diversity of the nineties may prompt corporate responses that the activism of the sixties could not. As one Gannett executive said, "It has nothing to do with altruism or concern about society. It has to do with survival."[6]

In the competitive global market, the imperative is changing from affirmative action to managing diversity. Neither phrase is likely to be consistent with the short-term priorities of time-pressured organizations struggling to show immediate financial results.

Many in the labor force will not be ready for full participation in fishnet organizations. A two-track system is emerging, with an underclass of disproportionately minority workers performing whatever routine functions are left: "McJobs," as they are called in Generation X lingo.[7] The elite teams and teams of teams will be drawn from those who have the skills to perform in the electronic organization. It is unlikely that once the baby boomers have retired, there will be enough of this later generation to meet businesses' needs.

Furthermore, organizations may find themselves trying to sidestep the wrath of those who are disenfranchised. It is, as yet, inappropriate to refer to people in these straits as a "class." But though they are far from organized, their numbers are staggering. Their actions could affect organizations large and small, although how is not clear.

Businesses might be tempted simply to avoid this sad backwater of society with its simmering sense of despair, or pretend it does not exist. In many parts of the United States, such avoidance is still possible, but for most companies it will not remain so for long. The stakes are rising for minorities, for companies with a serious interest in making the most of diversity in the workforce, for independent contractors, and for society at large.

The future could easily resemble that depicted in the film *Blade Runner:* in an underworld of constant drizzle, overwhelmed by gigantic electronic billboards, thrives a polyglot culture of thieves and killers with no access to the world of light above. Keeping such conditions hidden from sight is dangerous indeed.

13

Long-Distance, Cross-Cultural Management

Imagine what a NASA mission would be like without mission control. Today, many corporate astronauts are rocketing into market space as if they were launched from Cape Canaveral with no Houston base. Corporations have emphasized equipping their astronauts so that they can survive in hostile environments and do their telework, but they have given little thought to the ground crew.

As one planner for a major pharmaceutical company told us, "Our astronauts are out there doing deals, but we don't have anyone back home to process the deals they do! We're bound to have some disappointed customers, not to mention the astronauts themselves, who feel they have been cut off and left to drift in space."

New technologies can turn from status symbol to ball and chain overnight. As the dispersed fishnet organization expands around the globe, managers' need to maintain contact (read *control*) increases. The macho Road Warriors who at first enjoyed the status of having to be electronically accessible at all times (the ones whose modems were bigger than their computers) will come to resent the level of involvement and control those tools of long-distance management allow.

Carrying a pager once conferred status. It was the symbol of a very important person who had to stay in touch with the world. As pagers became commonplace, gardeners, janitors, and other service people began carrying them (not to speak of drug dealers and the like). Pagers can symbolize either freedom or a choke collar, depending on the role you are playing and how the pager fits into it.

Conditions demand that global organizations be simultaneously centralized and decentralized in various parts of their businesses. This is no longer an either/or choice that allows us to typecast a company easily. On the contrary, far-flung, geographically dispersed organizations may remain centralized for some important business functions. Like the individual, the company must figure out how to communicate in such a way that centralization and decentralization are both possible.

Diversity introduces a series of challenges to people who must move from one team to another. The mixes of co-workers on each new team in fishnet organizations will vary wildly, making a rainbow of colors, practices, and beliefs. Part of thinking globally is developing an openness to people from backgrounds different from our own. The increasing diversity of the world forces us to acknowledge and include cultural variety. This very openness, however, can allow cultural misunderstandings to proliferate.

Sam Adamson, president of a household-name corporation based in the United States, made a valiant effort to deal with the issue of diversity. His large manufacturing company was in the throes of hard times. Layoff fever was in the air. Rumors swept up from the factory floor and lofted back down again from the cubicles of middle management. Productivity slowed to an erratic trickle. Sales were off. Inventory was up. The prospects were not good unless something dramatic was done.

To counter the malaise, Sam hired a group of management consultants to help reengineer the corporation. Their vision was attractive, and it seemed that the corporation had a good chance of making it if it underwent radical change. Sam was certainly ready, and many of the employees were, too. But falling morale ran deeper than the nationwide economic slowdown. It was a nagging epidemic, infecting the whole company. It was impossible to talk seriously about reengineering with the majority of the workers in this mood. Radical restructuring could work only if Sam had people on his side, pulling together instead of pulling the company apart.

The consultants suggested that it might be helpful if the employees discussed their complaints and concerns about the current mood as well as their suggestions for the future. One consultant had a very creative idea: why not use the corporation's extensive electronic network as a way of bringing employees together?

So Sam called an "electronic town hall" meeting and opened it to employees in his division. For one week the company messaging system would provide an open forum for grievances and suggestions, not necessarily in that order. Sam thought employees might be more willing to vent their feelings if their comments were anonymous. The idea was primarily to give them a release, but some useful suggestions might also come out of the experiment.

The bold event got off to a bad start. Sam had scarcely sent out the e-mail announcement of the rules when the first angry messages began flying. A few responses in turn denounced the sudden attacks. The messages were all anonymous, of course. The next day Sam's in basket was filled with messages; printed out, they approached the size of the Manhattan phone book within five days. Sam assigned a team to organize the ideas into categories and make sense out of the wide-ranging and often contradictory criticisms. He would scan the new messages each night, before he went to sleep. He didn't sleep well.

By noon on the fourth day he was sweating profusely. There were complaints about "outside hotshots" telling people what to do, taking over or eliminating people's jobs. Those complaints were understandable, even predictable. But there were also complaints that unqualified women in management positions (identified sometimes by name, sometimes by unflattering characteristics) were abusing their power "just because they were women." Someone wrote in all capital letters that unqualified disabled workers were slacking off and getting special privileges. Complaints built on complaints; accusations built on accusations.

Themes did emerge. Most were unpleasant and strident. A variety of explosive topics came up, some with only very loose connections to the work environment: racism, sexism, nepotism, animal rights issues, abortion. There was little direct discussion of the reengineering effort except as a trigger for the explosion.

By early afternoon on the seventh day, Sam had loosened his tie and opened the collar of his lightly starched shirt, an action noted by the four managers who were reading the messages with him. But Sam, committed to making the process work, valiantly struggled on. By now most of the organization seemed to be involved in the electronic meeting, and messages were scrolling across the screen as fast as the network could put them there.

Work was at a standstill while one entire division of the corporation carped. Though the message senders were anonymous, names of specific employees were often mentioned, sometimes in very negative, even potentially libelous, ways.

Desperately, Sam pulled his keyboard to the edge of his desk. "Stop. This is not a reasonable exchange of views," he typed. "This meeting was to air grievances and ease our transition into the future. We want to hear from everyone, but not with name-calling, accusations, and slander."

A flood of electronic catcalls drowned out the president's plea. Sam glanced at the brass nameplate on his desk, realizing that the power he felt in his office meant little in the new electronic space he had created. A mob mentality had developed in this cool electronic medium. He was amazed. "This sure as hell ain't e-mail," Sam muttered.

Finally he ordered his network administrator to close down the electronic town hall. "My God," he breathed in frustration. "The corporation could be legally liable! I expected diversity, but this was more like ripping open a wound than beginning a constructive process of change!"

The four managers could only nod mutely. The experiment had been an unqualified disaster. Things were, if anything, worse than before. The consultants were fired, but even that did not make people feel much better. New consultants, of course, replaced them, and the reengineering went ahead.

It was not merely a media mismatch that undid Sam's efforts; it was a failure to recognize an entire complex of volatile cultural patterns. For Sam, and others in similar situations, the stress of trying to bridge cultures in the workplace often makes itself felt in symptoms like stomach distress, anger at others who are perceived as behaving in unreasonable ways, and a sense of frustration that nothing seems to be getting done. (The definition of "getting something done" also tends to vary across cultures, as does the definition of "how things work.")

The difficulties of organizing cross-cultural work intensify when businesses go global. Breakdowns occur more quickly when the "other side" is thousands of miles away and there are few common points of reference on which to build. This is especially true in acquisition or merger situations, where there are no shared corporate values. Even within strong corporate cultures, values are rarely strong or homogeneous enough to override cultural differences.

Confusion caused by language barriers is the most obvious, but beliefs about proper behavior and courtesy also shift across cultural lines. Americans, for example, because they value organization and method, accept having to stand in lines and are used to it. Not long ago, we were waiting in line at a ticket window in a medium-sized Italian city when a man who was obviously in a hurry cut to the front of the line, pushed his money at the clerk, and ordered—and received—his ticket. Clearly, the principle of "first come, first served," almost sacred to Americans, is not inviolable in Italian culture. What would have been rude behavior in our culture was completely natural in his. Such disparities are common across cultures.

Many managers, promoted to international positions because of their skills in getting things done, have come to realize how cross-cultural settings make their jobs much more difficult than before. With strong pressures from senior management to deliver on their business objectives, managers who do not know what to do to meet these new challenges will feel the stress, and lots of it.

Often when people from varied cultures are involved in a particular team, managers have assumed that team members will somehow work out among themselves how to communicate across cultural gaps in an efficient and effective manner. This is a dubious assumption.

Perry Wilcox was a member of an international team of engineers working on the design of a new manufacturing plant to be built in Italy. His office looked out on the other skyscrapers of downtown Dallas and beyond to the open Texas skies, now gathering ominous early morning clouds that would turn into afternoon storms. Pulling his gaze inside, Perry realized he was nervously rolling and unrolling a set of ragged plans on his desk while he waited for his call to Italy to go through.

It happened every time he talked with Italy: Something about transatlantic calls made him nervous. Luigi Cirasola, the architect with whom Perry had to coordinate the project, spoke fluent English, but at times Perry could barely understand his fast-talking Milanese accent. He spoke as if his words were falling behind his thinking, and his thinking was taking place in some twilight zone between Italian and English. His style could not have been more different from Perry's slow, deliberate manner of speaking.

When he finally heard Luigi's jaunty *"Pronto"* over the speaker phone, Perry felt a quick pang of fear that Luigi might think he was a countryman and would start firing Italian at him. But then Luigi said, "Hello, Perry. How're things in Dallas?" and he sighed with relief.

"Listen, Luigi," he said in his slow way, getting right down to business. "I'm calling about the revisions on the warehouse and loading dock. The gas storage facilities were right next to the fuel depot, and we have to move one or the other."

"Sure, sure. I know that, Perry. We're already working on it. We got the fax, don't worry. No problem. Yes. Yes."

Again Perry felt relief flood through him. His team included designers in Korea, draftsmen in Brazil, two process engineers in Boston, and a facilities developer on site in Torino. Any delay would cost the project days of effort and thousands, even hundreds of thousands, of dollars. So he took a deep breath and asked, "So, Luigi, can the plans be done in three weeks?"

Luigi didn't hesitate. "Sure," he said. "Three weeks, that's possible, sure. Yes."

After going over a range of other topics, Perry hung up. His tension had evaporated: a sticky international coordination problem was resolved.

But three weeks later there were no plans. There were still no plans after four weeks. So Perry, this time snapping the old rolled plans on the edge of his desk angrily, called Luigi again. "Where are the plans?" he asked, concealing his anxiety beneath brusqueness.

"Plans? What plans?"

"The plans you said you'd get to us in three weeks, Luigi. That was four weeks ago. The people in São Paulo are waiting. The clock is running and it's costing us money."

"I never said I'd send plans in three weeks. You asked me if it was possible to get the revisions on the warehouse done in three weeks, and I said it was possible. But you never said you wanted me to do it. We have other priorities here. Yes."

Perry groaned. This misunderstanding had cost the project a month, and it wasn't the first serious delay. Obviously, yes in Milan meant something quite different from yes in Dallas. Perhaps, Perry thought, the company should have invested some time and effort in that touchy-feely team-building stuff. Before he was laid off, the manager who was originally supposed to run this project had suggested a special effort at orientation and establishing trust among the globally dispersed participants. He was trying to sell them on the Team Performance Model. They should have listened. (See Figure 13-1.)

In this instance, the Italians had not done something that the Americans felt they had agreed to do. It turned out that Luigi had not understood it was an assignment; he had merely felt compelled to agree rather than raise questions. The delay and frustration caused by this episode characterized the whole project.

The work process for this cross-cultural team gradually improved, but only through trial and error by the engineers and architects involved, self-proclaimed bunglers at group dynamics. This pain is typical of today's cross-cultural teams: work does not get done on time and participants feel that they are not working well together but don't know why. If pressed for reasons, each culture blames the other. The work atmosphere is suffused with a simmering sense of disappointment.

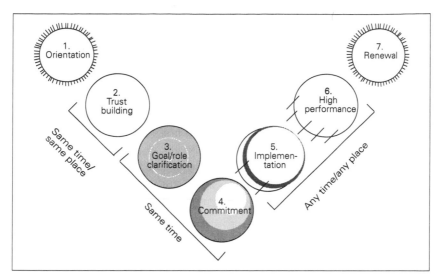

Figure 13-1 Team Performance™ Model, developed by David Sibbet and Allan Drexler (The Grove International, San Francisco), matched with optimum meeting options (see Figure 4-1 on page 26).

The mix-up with Luigi started Perry thinking. On this particular project, the problems he had confronted stemmed from the gap between international cultures, but it occurred to him that this case was merely an obvious instance of a much deeper cross-cultural problem, one he encountered a hundred times every day. Culture was not simply language and national identity; it included the myriad small, individual differences between areas of expertise and their diverse values, motives, needs, and goals. When he talked with someone who specialized in marketing, for example, he was working in a cross-cultural situation.

Often the mixing of cultures brings together people not only from different parts of the globe, but from different professional worlds or socioeconomic classes, of different genders, religions, ages, and sexual orientations, and having different physical challenges (for example, deaf people have their own distinct culture). Meetings of engineers and marketing representatives can involve as many problems of cross-cultural communication as when Japanese and American businesspeople try to work together. In spite of the growing necessity for cross-cultural cooperation on projects and increased openness to cultural variables in business, specific approaches to working across cultures are haphazard in most companies. Most companies today provide cross-cultural training only if an employee will be living abroad as part of an assignment. Typically, people working on cross-cultural teams are given no training whatsoever.

14

Remembering, Learning, Forgetting: The Lapse of Corporate Continuity

The evolving fishnet organization implies on-the-job mistakes. Accepting one's limitations and recognizing the continuing need to learn are prerequisites to good performance. Learning all you need to learn before you need to use it is increasingly impossible.

Problems arise around both the quantity of information to be learned and the quality of access to that information. The interlinked economy progresses at a staggering rate. Information doubles worldwide at ever-decreasing intervals. In 1950 it took sixteen years for information processing to double. In 1990 it was doubling every year. It is likely that the rate will be down to every month or even more often by 2025.[1]

The result is that employees constantly need to learn more while the time available for learning is shrinking. Just-in-time learning puts considerable pressure on organizations to figure out what training to provide when, and where. There are also new pressures on individuals, including both personal and psychological stresses.

Chris Argyris, who has studied organizations and learning for years, observed that highly educated consultants often have difficulty facing up to their own learning needs. "As long as efforts at learning and change focused on external organizational factors—job redesign, compensation programs, performance reviews, and leadership training—the professionals were enthusiastic participants.... And yet the moment the quest for continuous improvement turned to the professionals' own performance, something went wrong."[2] Argyris talks about a "doom loop" his well-motivated subjects went into when their performance was questioned. They developed a "brittleness" that made it very hard for them to accept their own personal need to learn, even though they had no trouble accepting the need for organizational learning.

A new breed of managers must accept ongoing learning as part of their job, but just-in-time learning won't work unless individuals accept their own need for it. Fishnet organizations made up of brittle people will break.

Once upon a time there was organizational memory. A broken organization not only can't learn what it needs to know; it forgets what it is, what it was, its mission and goals.

In the organizational hierarchy of the past, middle managers were the people who remembered things, who passed on corporate culture. When answers were needed, they were the ones who would know what to do based on their experience. Without those who have used information in the past and know how to get to it again, information itself gets lost. Middle managers also remembered the details of work processes, how to get things done, which is often as important as remembering information. (See Figure 7-1 on page 38.)

Middle managers worked at keeping the organization in sync. They functioned as the living and growing memory banks for the entire corporation. Now that many middle managers are gone, such functions, if they are fulfilled at all, are served in a very different way. Departing managers are taking corporate memory with them. Turnover and organizational turmoil result in spotty organizational memory and therefore spotty business support. A financial services executive recently stated, "All our downsizing clients are complaining that as the middle managers leave, they take essential knowledge with them. They were the people who knew how to wind up the clocks. " As middle managers disperse into the interlinked economy and participate on multiple teams, corporate memory, like a fragmented hologram, loses its shape.

Meanwhile the filing cabinets and data archives of corporate America are flushed with increasing frequency as the fear of subpoenas and lawsuits encourages companies to purge their memories. The motto of corporate lawyers seems to be, Shred early and often. A typical retention limit for business information is now about three months. As one software designer said, "You can't sell something called 'organizational memory' to American companies. The lawyers won't let you."

Co-workers frequently report poor group memory between meetings of project teams; team members don't always remember who agreed to do what, or otherwise differ on details. They make old mistakes because they can't remember what they or other groups learned before.

In addition, the time pressures of the information era are driving companies to look for new ways to work faster and smarter. For this we need new approaches to meeting support. When *meeting* meant individuals coming together in a room, a physical space, the social skills associated with the personality-driven manager were appropriate. Persuasion, leadership, the ability to build consensus, and salesmanship were all effective qualities that are now receding in importance in an era when information comes not only from meeting presentations but from a dizzying array of on-line services, CD-ROM databases, and electronic communications channels as well.

In such an environment, information overload is a real danger. The threat is as if a garbage truck had overturned and dumped wilted intellectual lettuce on bystanders. The consequences of haste can be too much memory or too much useless memory, as well as too little memory.

Americans have always had a penchant for action solutions, and the quest for a new business order is following the troubling tradition of salvation in a buzzword. The prophets of reengineering (mostly the consultants who sell it) claim that fortunes can be made by abandoning the types of operations that have evolved over the years in large organizations and leaping to streamlined modes of operation facilitated by new technology.

Most reengineering envisions a dispersed, network-style organization that emphasizes business processes, which in turn require more continuity than ever. At the adventurous end of the spectrum are organizations like Chiat Day, the large advertising firm that is eliminating personal offices and going "virtual." Professionals are given portable computers and sent to figure out on their own how this new arrangement is supposed to work. On the more conservative end are organizations like the insurance company in Canada that is reworking its entire customer operations in the hope of surviving a major consolidation of the industry that will eliminate many companies in the next few years.

The move toward reengineering, redesign, or similar reinventions of business processes, is being fueled by a number of different interests. Financiers and investors hope for greater profits through increased productivity. Managers envision work that "flows" with more efficiency if workers are "empowered" to solve problems themselves. Consultants see a chance to bring about fundamental change—and make a lot of money. Software designers and technology companies imagine technotopias of collaboration and communication, all augmented, of course, by the new devices they are producing. Work flow means cash flow.

The loss of continuity and corporate memory, however, cannot easily be restored. Each new scheme that purports to solve the problem of preserving institutional memory has its own disciples, associations, literature, distinctions, success stories. Each also has a slightly different language for describing similar phenomena. This is an area rife with conflicting approaches, and haggling over terminology is common. The search for continuity is impeded by the very efforts to pursue it.

Acquiring and maintaining a sense of place and personhood in this fluid environment is a challenge. Self-esteem and self-worth, the ability to accept praise and support, and a sense of the continuity of the self are the offspring of this evolutionary change in business culture. As in cross-cultural contexts, language itself sometimes appears to be at risk as the organizations that supported the flow of goods and services in the past fragment, form and re-form in ever-new configurations. Just as middle managers must make their way in the new business environment, so too the organizations they have left, and the ones they will work with in partnership, will have to find their path.

Unfortunately for the former middle manager who is burning her severance pay, points of reference that were available in the corporation of the past are gone, and the new global, interlinked, electronic infrastructure of the future is still being built. Everyone is on his own. There are few precedents, little context from which workers can learn the key to business survival.

Continuity is the context of business processes. It is the pace at which things work, played out in real time. It is a succession or flow of events to make a coherent whole.

Continuity gives both individuals and institutions a sense of connection with both the past and the future and an identity that is constantly evolving through time. History provides a context, an imprint in the matrix of memory. Without it individuals and corporations have nothing to distinguish themselves from others and must continually scramble to re-create and maintain a sense of where they are in their marketplace.

Reengineering and restructuring have left many of today's corporations, especially the large ones, filled with gaps in their structure and lapses in their continuity. Some large corporations are now so filled with holes that they have little sense of themselves as complete entities.

Without continuity a company becomes lost, unsure of what it is. If everyone working for a corporation forgot each morning the history of the organization, where it started and how far it has come, along with its procedures and its webs of relationships with customers, suppliers, competitors, vendors and among internal departments, the company would no longer exist. It would evaporate in institutional amnesia.

15

Banana-Now Time

Reengineering and redesign often focus on time compression. Many reengineering efforts are like forcing fruit, compressing the plant production process to speed up the time to harvest. Product development cycles are too long: they must be shortened to be competitive. Urgency—what we call the Federal Express effect—drives everything: somebody is always willing to get a package to your customer anywhere in the world in two days, one day, even twelve hours. There is no longer any handy excuse for not responding to a request by the next business day, if not immediately by fax or electronic mail. Faster, faster, faster yet; hurry or lose the race. There is no time to reflect when the pressure is on just to respond.

This this problem is partly the result of our very success. Technology has changed the world. Whereas business communication used to rely chiefly on the mails and the office telephone, we now have overnight mail, fax machines, e-mail, and cellular phones. The dimensions of time have shriveled to a wink. The old structures are not only inadequate to meet our communications needs; they *cannot* function as they once did.

But such thinking can produce temporal tunnel vision. The time horizon is already close and getting closer. We can't see beyond it, so we think nothing is there.

Everyone in business knows what time is: it's money. The less time spent on providing a product or service, the greater the profit.

In the wake of restructuring and reengineering, attitudes toward time itself are changing. Time is growing indefinite, its substance insubstantial. Institutions that only a few years ago seemed stable, enduring, eternal (and so outside of time) are fading in unreliable memory. Giant corporations like IBM, Eastman Kodak, General Motors,

AT&T, and so on were once perceived as permanent structures, continuing even as the people who formed them came and went. The passage of those who contributed to making the corporate legacy was marked by the gold retirement watch. (Curiously, the fewer years the recipient likely had left in his lifetime, the greater the value of the watch.)

Workers used to be rewarded for long-term employment; now they are often punished for it. Large corporations have discovered, to their surprise, that they too, like the human beings who are their substance, have a finite lifespan: birth, flourishing, reproduction, decline.

In the aftermath of reengineering, we have a chance to rethink our attitudes toward time and how we use it. To begin, we must realize that our assumptions about time may need to change in the new organizational climate. Metaphorically, do we really know what time it is? We must get to know time again, the "familiar stranger," as J. T. Fraser, founder of the International Society for the Study of Time, calls it.[1]

Most businesses still measure time as if with a stop watch. The Wall Street notion of time is focused on immediate results, as reflected in quarterly earnings statements, and the charting of business cycles, measured in days or weeks or months.

Fraser warns that our broader awareness of time can easily slip back to the level of animals. If our connection with the world around us is overly biotemporal—the mentality Fraser calls "banana-now" time, that of biological processes—we lose the rich perspective that is ours as thinking and feeling human beings. Chimpanzees and apes think only of the banana they want right now, not about the banana an unborn grandchild might eat or the banana consumed last month. Preoccupation solely with immediate concerns can be dangerous to our humanity: "If in our individual and collective behavior we were to let our mental present deteriorate to a 'banana-now' present . . . then we should lose the very capacity that built human civilizations. We should become the time-zombies of a banana-now republic."

The "bottom-line" attitude that still tends to dominate business thinking, driven by balance sheet results and quarterly reports, restricts our temporal vision to banana-now time. "It is a trend, observable around the globe," Fraser says, "towards favoring stopgap measures in preference to seeking long-term solutions to socioeconomic problems."[2]

In the maelstrom of postmodern global business, where chaos is always hovering just beyond the edge of vision and where there is the constant threat posed by stagnation, awareness of time presents a constant challenge.

A consequence of setting our watches to banana-now time is, for example, the urgency with which participants regard meetings that are not about issues vital to a business's well-being but rather about territorial imperatives. Who controls a meeting becomes more important than the goal of the meeting. Fallen beyond the banana-now time horizon, long-term objectives are forgotten.

Writer and educator George Leonard has described some of the dangers of a foreshortened perspective on time. The most pervasive and insidious is a peculiarly American phenomenon: the drive for immediate solutions. "The quick-fix, antimastery mentality," Leonard writes, "touches almost everything in our lives. Look at modern medicine and pharmacology. 'Fast, temporary relief' is the battle cry. Symptoms receive immediate attention; underlying causes remain in the shadows."[3]

Reengineering can be a quest for the quick fix, for both employers and employees. The problem worsens with the relentless financial pressures for immediate performance in the short run. Wall Street insists on winning now, today, this minute, and has little memory of the past or reflective anticipation of the future. In most Silicon Valley companies, "a long time" is defined as three months—about the same length of time files are maintained—punctuated by the quarterly report. How can a company define and organize around a long-term vision if results must be measured within just a few months? In Japanese businesses, "a long time" is measured in years, or even decades.

It is no secret that memory grows short and uncertain under threat, but corporations, like individuals, need a long-term orientation in order to succeed. A short-term time horizon creates a tendency to bounce from crisis to crisis, without ever getting a sense of the long view or the strategic alternatives. And a time of crisis is usually poor-quality time.

Our children tell us that what gives time with them its quality is an intensity of attention. Without attention, time lacks quality. Small amounts of time with great attention are far preferable to great amounts of time with little attention.

In a time-compacted globe, where the nomads of the night have colonized every corner of the calendar and the clock, a notion like "quality" seems quaint, properly belonging to the domestic realm, the "soft" side of life. Quality made up of such attention has no place on the battlefield people call the business world. There simply isn't enough time for it.

In the fourteenth century, books were written to last. Anything of only momentary interest was delegated to broadsheets or handbills. Today, of course, as Fraser points out, "the emphasis is on the best-seller now, not on the long seller for decades or centuries to come."[4]

Quality used to mean something well-made, crafted with the attention of a master, one who had spent a lifetime perfecting the art. It meant something fitted closely to its purpose, or something deliciously apt.

Who determines quality after reengineering? It is only through human beings that quality takes on its meaning. Artists may determine quality for themselves—how well a work fits its conception—but for the art to have cultural meaning, someone else must appreciate it.

The current business emphasis on quality assumes that attention is important, yet it inverts the traditional relation of time to quality. It used to be that the longer it took to make something, the more quality it possessed, and the higher price it could command. The relationship of time to quality is changing. Perceptions of time are contracting; an analogy to the trend in solid-state circuitry is kicking in, dictating that faster as well as smaller is better. Time has often become a countervailing force against quality.

In today's business world, product development cycles, customer service procedures, and other time-consuming activities must grow ever shorter. The pace becomes more frantic as companies move toward an ideal of "just in time." Time must be compressed, but without sacrificing quality. Time itself therefore demands more attention, not less, with a great deal of focus.

One layoff victim we interviewed called a former colleague who had survived the cut at his company. Fred was on vacation when the layoffs were announced. He was called back from his holiday on an emergency basis. His first day back in the office, his boss announced that Fred was to have a state-of-the-art cellular phone installed in his car—which happened to be a rusted 1983 Volvo with 210,000 miles on it. The next week Fred was issued a pager to make him even more quickly accessible to meet his boss's requests, which began to arrive in the evenings and on weekends, always with a demand for immediate response.

Has the quality of Fred's work improved? Has the quality of the corporation's product increased? What about the quality of Fred's life?

And how might Fred compare his situation to that of his laid-off colleague, who became a free-lance entrepreneur?

The trade-off, as Fraser remarks, is between freedom and coherence. Dr. Johnson's *Dictionary of the English Language* was published almost a century and a half after Shakespeare had created a standard of quality for written English. Before it appeared, spelling had always been idiosyncratic (free); now *orthography* ("right" or "true" writing) had to be uniform to be understood. Shakespeare himself had had no notion that there was a single "correct" way of spelling his own name. Once the dictionary was available, society gained in cohesion because anyone could refer to it as an outside source for comparison. Fraser observes, "With that step toward more precise communication, the individual lost some of his freedom, while the community gained an added degree of coherence."[5]

As time compresses in the emerging global environment, such standardization is increasingly important, despite the loss of freedom it entails. Industry groups everywhere are meeting to hammer out standards for data compression, digital video file structures, interoperability, communications protocols on the Internet. Computers, and the underlying communications network that supports them, have been a powerful force for such standardization. Spell checkers are one modest application of the trend toward global standardization.

Here's where flexible organizations driven by business teams may run into a rub, however. Organizations and business teams must be able to respond to short-term feedback, which makes it more difficult to promote long-range perspectives. Often dominated by temporary suborganizations, the fishnet organization is faced with the strong temptation to cut corners on quality for the sake of short-term returns. Who is responsible for long-term performance? What happens when hoshins, long-range goals, meet the here and now?

For some American companies, this has already occurred. In today's business climate, the here and now generally wins. The total quality folks become layoff victims, although they are often in demand at other corporations that are at different stages in the reengineering cycle.

Reengineering often involves a radical rethinking of all business operations. The middle manager, newly freed from traditional tasks, has only to look around to see that the future lies outside any organization that is out of step with the new temporal rhythm. New structures, and with them new concepts of quality, are forming despite what we may want. It suddenly seems as if release from enduring loyalties to the large organization (and the loss of security and identity that implies) also allows the weight of history to be shed.

Total quality implies a long-term perspective, but business teams are sucked into immediacy. The new manager will not be so constrained. We must all take responsibility for our own lives, for their quality and flavor. Though the greater reliance on business teams is a step in the right direction, teams too can often find it difficult to resist the quick-fix approach. Carried along by crack business teams, flexible organizations can create things on the fly and are capable of major innovations in what are, by the standards of traditional organizations, short time periods. Their innovations, however, may be limited by their short-term orientation. Staccato innovations that are flashy but do not run deep will be most common. Many quick-fix innovations can also have negative business implications in the long run.

The fortress organization is gone, and the fishnet organization has not yet taken shape. The rules and structures that will regulate and reward work at home and with diverse co-workers are in an embryonic stage. Few managers understand the ramifications of global time and temporal cycles. Without attention, the future could easily brew sour, disaffected, discouraged workers and dysfunctional organizations.

With the right kind of attention, however, we, as individuals and as organizations, can take charge of the future. We can find and align ourselves in a new, more hopeful, more satisfying, and more rewarding community. We can become what we never were before.

III

REBUILDING AND
THE QUEST FOR
CONTINUITY

What could be: Creating opportunities for yourself
and your organization, now and in the future

16

Opportunities for
Fishnet Organizations

Schwab Architecture and Migration Strategy is the new fishnet information system for the discount brokerage house Charles Schwab. The old system was located in a single central processor on one floor of a building in earthquake-prone San Francisco. The new system processes customer orders and communications across more than 135 Schwab offices. Processing operations are more secure in the event of emergencies, and customers can get more complete responses from local offices. Mark Barmann, chief information officer for Schwab during the conversion, characterized the former system this way: "Our business processes were almost like fused pieces of plastic stuck together to form a rigid whole that resisted change."[1]

Fishnets are not made out of hard plastic, for good reason. Before the change, Barmann led a needs assessment study to look at what was going on in Schwab's offices. The study identified twenty-four underlying business processes, what Barmann calls "the business in Lego form," which then became the core of the new system.

You cannot make a fishnet out of Lego blocks either, but their interlinked, modular form is a quality you can make good use of in rethinking business structures. Schwab is reengineering its own business in one visionary leap that will require six years to execute. Others have taken smaller, more evolutionary steps that are still quite dramatic.

Rosenbluth Travel is a small company that has grown into an electronically facilitated fishnet organization that is both centralized and decentralized. Over the past ten years, the company's annual sales have grown from $40 million to more than $1 billion. Based in Philadelphia, this family-owned business now has more than three hundred offices in the United States, plus associations (through Rosenbluth International Alliance) with thirty other agencies in thirty-three countries, adding over one thousand global locations. The alliance structure allows great flexibility to gear up or down, yet promotes a spirit of partnership that not only encourages high performance but provides corporate identity and shared rewards.

Eric Clemons is a leading analyst of corporate strategy at the Wharton School at the University of Pennsylvania who has extensively studied Rosenbluth Travel over the past few years. Clemons concludes that the company's success is based on its exploitation of the discontinuities and uncertainties following airline deregulation in 1978 along with its heavy and creative use of information technologies. Clemons also emphasizes the importance of "vision and hustle"—the company's ability not just to make simple business choices, but to create opportunity out of challenges.[2]

At the beginning of this period of expansion, Hal Rosenbluth demoted himself and spent two years as a reservations clerk to get a bottom-up perspective on his business. He learned that "the public was confused. No one knew what airfares were available. That's when we realized we were in the information business, not just the travel business."[3] Rosenbluth focused on the market in corporate travel and came up with such innovations as listing flights by fare instead of the standard listing by time of departure, which required an agent to look across different screens and make decisions based on whatever fares appeared. This innovation is a good example of what Stan Davis calls "informationalizing" business: figuring out what information might add value to an existing product or service, and providing it for a price.[4] Rosenbluth went on to introduce a series of further changes:

- a database of client information that allowed travel clerks to personalize services;

- an electronic transactions tracking system that compiled a wide range of travel data, letting customers analyze their travel patterns more closely; and

- guaranteed savings programs through partnerships with corporate clients (rather than competition based directly on price, which was the industry norm).

By transforming itself in fundamental ways, Rosenbluth Travel became an outstanding business success. At the same time it was also forced to confront great uncertainty in its marketplace, with real threats to its traditional business. Hal Rosenbluth was not fazed by the unsure implications of airline deregulation: "What did deregulation mean? We weren't sure we knew. But if all the bets were off, the company that could gather information faster and turn it into knowledge would win."[5]

The company's goal was quick response time in the turbulent travel industry. Growing programs like the Rosenbluth International Alliance are rooted in principles like competing on quality of service rather than price.

When Rosenbluth Travel set up the first corporate travel reservation center in the country and embarked on an aggressive plan to use information technology to create new products and services, its plan was visionary, risky, and expensive. As David Miller, vice president for global information technology, said, "We did not just automate the old way of doing business."[6] Such a leap of faith required intuition about where the marketplace was going and confidence in how the company's core skills could make a difference. Rosenbluth Travel redefined its business by creating new information services that were attractive to its corporate customers.

Even in retrospect, Hal Rosenbluth does not claim to have known just what he was going to do. The company dealt with uncertainty through a flexible organizational style, aided by a rapidly evolving information network. Rosenbluth brought a sense of continuity to a chaotic industry, and his customers bought it.

Language Line, a fishnet organization of another kind, began out of the need of hospitals and police in the San Jose area for translation services in order to communicate with patients and citizens in emergencies. Now owned by AT&T, which offers it as a basic service, Language Line provides language translation over the telephone, serving clients throughout the country in 147 different languages. Translators, most of whom work from their homes all around the United States, handle requests as they come in. The company's small main office is in Monterey, California, and there are a few regional centers where translators work together at the same site, but the organization is really located on the telephone network, not in an office building.

Language Line is a virtual company, one that exists because of its electronic capabilities and that could not function without the flexibility of people working from their homes. The Language Line concept lets everyone win: the customers, who get on-demand access to translators; the translators, who appreciate having skilled jobs they can do at home, with flexible hours; and AT&T, which is reaping the profits of the service.

Business consultants William Davidow and Michael Malone write about one of the oldest continuously operating corporations in the world, the small-arms manufacturer Beretta, founded in 1492, as an example of how a company can adapt new technologies to its own uses.[7] Today Beretta uses CAD software to design new products, then electronically transfers the instructions for computer-integrated manufacturing to regional factories, bypassing the company's own factory floor to bring the product closer to the customer. The result is a virtual structure that spans the globe.

Such companies are leaving the traditional trappings of corporate existence behind. In the process, buildings and capital equipment and departments like finance and payroll vanish from the books. Interlinked, cooperative enterprises, extending and growing globally, weave purely mental structures. More and more of an organization's existence inhabits virtual space: the on-off bits of computer memory, and the beliefs and imaginations of the people who forge that memory. This creates a need for a new corporate essence as well.

Innovative companies are willing to spend money to make money, but the information era will require a special brand of vision. New information technologies can help cable up the fishnet organization to make things happen that were not possible before. It will be expensive, but such innovation will lead to new business opportunities.

Fishnets must be flexible enough to include teams working in anytime/anyplace work spaces, whose members are characterized by ethnic, gender, class, and national diversity. Workers in the new organization must continue to learn new skills, and they must be able to foster a psychological sense of continuity. Finally, attention to both quality and efficiency is essential. Winning companies, and the free-lance contractors who will make up an increasing proportion of their workforce, will be ones who grow responsively and responsibly.

Not all the changes will be pleasant or easy. Conflict persists. The question is not how to eliminate conflict, but how to manage it. The postmodern descendants of the Organization Man are not victims, after all, but pioneers.

As science writer William Poundstone has remarked, "Most great advances in science come when a person of insight recognizes common elements in seemingly unrelated contexts."[8] The essence of management in fishnet organizations lies in riding out conflicts long enough to see the common elements in unrelated contexts and weave them together. This task is actually easier outside the old hierarchical corporate structure, where information was compartmentalized and unrelated contexts kept strictly separate.

A fundamental shift in the emerging essence of the fishnet organization is the recasting of problems as dilemmas. A problem is an obstacle to be overcome, a border that impedes passage along a linear notion of time, which proceeds endlessly from the past, a point lost in antiquity, into the future, another point somewhere far ahead of us. Problems block our way. No sooner is one border crossed than another one appears just ahead.

By contrast, a dilemma is a balanced set of two alternatives, needs, or opportunities. A dilemma is like a frontier, harboring a chaotic mix of nonlinear forces that create new and often evanescent structures. A dilemma embodies difficult choices. An example is the choice whether to buy American- or foreign-made products. In the old mercantilist model of business, economic chauvinism required that people favor goods made by companies in their own country and not by foreign competitors. Now that the economy is global and increasingly interlinked, however, the old us-versus-them problem has become a complex dilemma. Is it better for the national economy if one buys a Honda manufactured in the United States or a Ford made in Mexico? It is a matter of finding a balance between the center and the periphery.

Dick Beckhard, a long-term pioneer of organizational development, maintains that, unlike problems, dilemmas are not solved but managed.[9] Organizational dilemmas will haunt the nineties, and there is no escape. Unfortunately, many managers still seek comfortable predictability, whether consciously or unconsciously. For this reason, many large corporations in the middle to late nineties will not be pleasant places to work, even for those who have survived the cuts in the workforce.

The "home office," with its old rigidities, can no longer function effectively. It can provide values, but it cannot control. This is uncomfortable for those used to the reassuring presence of a problem-solving mind-set. Finding the balance between allegiance to the local customer and allegiance to the home office is a dilemma, not a problem. Kenichi Ohmae says, "Brute force is neither necessary nor effective. A new form of organization, organic and amoebalike, makes that balance easier to achieve."[10]

Manufacturing companies have always had to choose among different products to develop. The choice was based on a determination of costs balanced against future revenue. This kind of decision making is no longer appropriate. "Product development . . . is a general investment for the future at a certain level of risk," Ohmae writes.[11] Living with risk means learning to manage dilemmas, which for most people demands a shift in attitude. Quantitative analysis, logic, and reason are less appropriate tools than flexibility without preconceptions.

In the martial arts of China and Japan, one's mental and spiritual attitude is more important than strength or technique. Discussion of what a proper spiritual attitude is is couched in metaphor. "A river of energy flows through the body," a master might say. "Allow the energy to pour out the fingertips without obstacle within or outside the body."

Such talk may sound like vague mysticism, but it can be a practical metaphor for a state of relaxed, nonthreatening alertness without tension, contrasting with the weight and force of a cumbersome organizational hierarchy in the traditional metaphor. Workers in fishnet organizations must figure out how to maintain this kind of balance. Managers who thrive in such organizations will be those with a high tolerance for ambiguity. They will be the kind of people who can wrestle with dilemmas, not simply those who can take a punch or two at problems. These are the managers who will be best prepared to meet the challenge of an uncertain future.

17

Anytime/Anyplace
Work: Use, Not Abuse

Twenty years after it first emerged as a possibility, anytime/anyplace work is becoming both popular and practical. Institutions, individual entrepreneurs, and globe-trotting knowledge workers are finally realizing that anytime/anyplace work *can* work.

Horror stories about the downside of anytime/anyplace work are increasingly rare. Nonetheless, a routine application of the anytime/anyplace idea, while it can improve efficiency, can yet have no influence on effectiveness. Novel applications, by contrast, can have broad results. For example, anytime/anyplace programs allow prison inmates to hold outside jobs. Such programs are already under way in California, New York, Arizona, and Minnesota. Anytime/anyplace work can be ideal for those needing to care for children or elderly parents. As the population ages, the need for adult children to care for older relatives at home will only increase. Unlike young children, elderly people usually do not need constant attention, but of course they still require occasional help or assistance in an emergency. Combinations of work at home and elderly care can, in many instances, be very attractive.

But the slope toward all-the-time/every-place work is slippery. The more possible it is to call on people anytime/anyplace, the more likely businesses are to overuse this new resource to quench their urgent thirst for time, and the more people will feel their private lives are being invaded. What workers gain in flexibility in the short run they could lose in increased workloads that fill every available moment: not just the time they used to spend commuting, but also evenings and

103

weekends at home that they used to have to themselves. Decentralization and its resulting centrifugal force have sent many managers reeling as well. As they and their employees spin out into the realms of anytime/anyplace work, they have found themselves in a world of overwork at home or on the road. Although some of this pressure is relieved by anytime/anyplace office technology, new stresses arise, at least for those at certain links in the chain of work.

The Institute for the Future, in a recent national survey, found that more than a third of all U.S. employees work a significant part of the time away from the office. These workers have a pressing need to set levels: what is the right balance of home versus office work for each corporation, each family, each manager? There are few guidelines at present. The emerging shape-shifting business organization remains intensely ambiguous. Like all dilemmas, the balance between home and office work must be judiciously managed.

Some innovative corporations and hardy entrepreneurs have struck out on their own, creating new business niches and new business processes that seem to work. Some on the edge of pioneering new work styles have been featured in breathy articles for the popular business press. Others have opted for multiple part-time careers, the quiet side of anytime/anyplace work.

Pilot projects in varied forms of telecommuting and remote work are critical, but it is growing late for pilots. By now, most large corporations should have programs in place, at least on a small scale. Delay at this point will mean a major catch-up—and cleanup—down the road. (See Figure 17-1.)

Corporations should be making systematic attempts to learn from the early experience of employees on the frontier of telecommuting. Telework is here to stay, even though teleworkers and their employers are still defining what it is. They do know it is most certainly not the simplistic notion of the electronic cottage-office as a routine substitute for the central office. Employers who rely on remote work must acknowledge the entire complex of behavior, emotion, and the meaning of what it is to be a human being in establishing remote work practices. More and more people seek a balance in their lives, even as pressures from work increase.

Martha Wagner is one of the everyday pioneers of love and work, and she has learned some practical rules of thumb. When she lost her job as a manager at a large engineering firm in 1989, she used the opportunity to go into business for herself. She had thought that she could attend to the needs of her two school-age daughters and fulfill

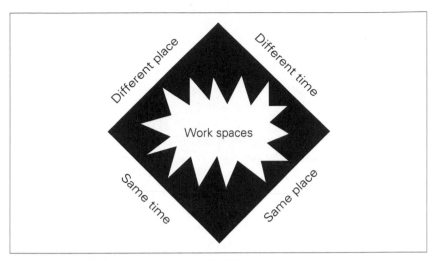

Figure 17-1 Work spaces must be flexible to business and personal needs, rather than compartmentalized

her career goals at the same time, but she quickly found unanticipated challenges in making the transition.

Over coffee on a sunny fall day in California she told us about her experiences working out of a home office. "One afternoon I got home from a business trip, and the first thing I did was check my voice mail. My kids, who were home from school, said, 'You don't have to go straight to your answering machine, Mom. You can wait until we're in bed.' And you know, they were right; my voice mail could wait a few hours. There was nothing critical there that couldn't wait until the next day, anyway. It was a revelation, and one that I learned directly from my kids."

Until recently, most employees of large American corporations have clearly defined the boundary between traditional work, the archetypal nine-to-five office job, and the rest of existence—home, family, and community life. The boundary was physical: work took place at a location distant from home, behind company walls, in architectural structures shaped and laid out in ways that differed from those of home and social life. The boundary was also temporal, with routine "office hours" allowing little deviation.

Today the boundary grows increasingly transparent. As if to make this very point, the doors to Martha's home office are glass. Even when she is working, she can see out of her office and those who inhabit the other part of her life can see in.

Martha discovered that a few simple rules about her home office are helping to maintain this porous and transparent border. When the doors are closed, for example, she is working, and her family knows she does not want to be disturbed. When she is not inside her office, she is not working, period: her answering machine handles the telephone; business can wait. If she is in her office but the door is open, her family knows that she is in the halfway zone of casual work at home and can be interrupted. The solution is not complete, but it helps to manage the dilemmas of working at home.

Such rules are only a beginning. The challenges of this new commingling of love and work are neither simple nor clear. One thing that is clear, however, is that the change from the defined work space and office hours to anytime/anyplace work is emotionally unsettling because of the breakdown of traditional categories. Guilt and anxiety are the most obvious effects on the worker. The expectations of employers, managers, and workers will have to adapt, along with the expectations of family members who share the lives of telecommuters.

The cutting edge of telework is in the basement of a small house on a tree-lined street in the tiny central Illinois town of Gridley. Eric lives upstairs with his wife and two small children, close to where his parents and grandparents live, in the community where he grew up. He has lived in Gridley his entire life, except for seven years he spent in Texas working for a large oil company.

Eric still works full-time for his Texas employer, but now his office is in his basement, a thousand miles from the home office in Texas. His workstation displays the same screen and electronic desktop he had in Texas. He has a video telephone on his desk and separate phone lines for fax and conference calls.

Eric hasn't even told his barber about the strange goings-on in his basement. Gridley does not yet have upgraded telephone services, and it is not at the top of anyone's list for exotic telework. Telluride or Santa Monica it is not. Three boring phone lines snake quietly under the front porch into Eric's wood-frame house.

The corporation has adopted a "buddy system" for telecommuters. Back in Texas, Bridgette, Eric's partner, brings a different set of skills and capabilities to their work as a team. Because Eric works in the basement of his house in Gridley, Illinois, he doesn't know what is going on in the Houston office as well as Bridgette, so she acts as a kind of Seeing Eye dog. For a while after Eric moved back to Illinois, Bridgette received many of the requests he used to get when he was in Texas. Gradually, though, people realized that he was as accessible as she was; he works the same hours and can be reached by phone, videophone, or computer messaging. Eric has become an invisible man around the office: though he can neither see nor be seen, he is very much present and accounted for. His workplace has become a work space. His body is rarely in Texas, but *he* is.

Can Eric and the thousands of teleworkers lining up behind him become career telecommuters? The answer appears to be a resounding yes. Another career planning option is being born. Given the requirements of the Clean Air Act that mandate a reduction in workers' commuting time, telework is no longer either a technological fantasy or an interesting pilot test funded by some phone company with a new network to sell. Anytime/anyplace work has become a legislative imperative and a practical possibility.

Star Enterprise (a partnership of Texaco and Saudi Refining, Inc.) has embarked on a program to telework much of their field marketing workforce. The pilot test of this initiative involves giving the nomadic field staff a laptop computer which is connected via ordinary phone lines to the traditional office local area network infrastructure. Using this connection, the nomad user has full access to needed information and information facilities which include operational data, financial measures, and e-mail type links. Use of the nomadic strategy means that the marketing field worker carries his office with him like a hermit crab carries his shell. An important by-product of this strategy is that expensive office space has been released and the required information is delivered to the mobile worker who now spends more time directly involved with his constituency.

Other companies have begun evaluating issues of work and family, but as yet very few in the United States have adopted explicit policies. Simple checklists help identify good candidates for telecommuting, but they tend to be narrow and conventional in an age in which options are changing rapidly. Goodwill abounds but there is a lack of good sense.

High-powered two-career couples who negotiate hard for arrangements that will balance the demands of work and family are likely to force a change in corporate policies. Even in the midst of the current job crisis, some skills are at a premium. Many of those who have these skills also have partners with comparable economic value. Such high-leverage couples will pave the way for new work/family policies. There are strong economic incentives for corporations to be responsive to employees' personal needs. Work/family programs are typically benevolent in intent but difficult to justify in business terms. Many corporations are willing to do good, but most want to do well at the same time.

We all work in a changing environment. Some may work regular hours but in different places; others may work in the same place every day but have erratic schedules. Co-workers may be a permanent team or a constantly shifting flux of diverse people. Developing guidelines for negotiating the terms of work is a high priority.

There are alternatives. Now is the time to begin experimenting. Groups like the Conference Board and the Families and Work Institute (both in New York City) have established exchanges on work/family topics, a useful forum for sharing learning and perspectives. Moving toward a human resource policy for anytime/anyplace work is not only the right thing to do to support our families and communities, but it is necessary for businesses' success in the long run.

18

Info-Mediation

$\mathbf{A}$rthur C. Clarke once said that any sufficiently advanced technology is indistinguishable from magic. While the promises of information technologies do sound like magic, the time-compressed global economy is impossible without telecommunications and computing and the people who make them work. Information technologies not only transfer knowledge from where it is stored to where it is needed; they filter, shape, and interpret that knowledge. Workers in fishnet organizations must understand the ways in which information technologies can mediate work so they can use them effectively and minimize the inevitable negative side effects.

The alternatives offered by technology for organizational communication, whether based on hardware or software, fall into three basic areas. They are person-to-person media (fax, voice mail, e-mail, telephone and videophone, document sharing), meeting support (video conferencing, desktop video meetings, electronic whiteboards), and the more exotic forms of meeting inside models or simulated spaces, known by the awkward expression "virtual reality." Because the first two areas are reasonably familiar, we will look most closely at the third in this quick overview of available technology.

Deciding among communications technologies involves not only knowing how they can facilitate work, but also how they can distort or mislead it. Three professors at the Harvard Business School have explored the future organization, forecasting its development over the next thirty years. A key conclusion: "The new technology is more powerful, more diverse, and increasingly entwined with the organization's critical business processes. Continuing to react to new technology and the organizational change it triggers could throw a business into a tailspin."[1]

Everyone in the new anytime/anyplace work space has confronted the "blizzard of lies" that shapes our daily discourse (see Chapter 9). What, we must ask ourselves, is the etiquette of the emerging business world? Perhaps phrases like "We'll send someone right out" and "We'll keep your name on file" aren't exactly lies after all. They may represent those small courtesy phrases that seem to mean something, but which everyone knows are placeholders to smooth awkward patches in social relationships. "We must have lunch" often does not mean what the words say; it is only intended to ease the transition of departure. "He's in a meeting now" is much the same, a face-saving method of avoidance.

The telephone is still the most basic medium for connections across a fishnet organization. Although global access is still a problem in some parts of the world, basic telephone service is getting better and cheaper. Meanwhile, both conference calling and video teleconferencing have grown to the point that they have become practical tools for every organization, not just those with large private networks. Audio and video teleconferencing each became billion-dollar businesses in 1993, and they are still growing.

It may be necessary from time to time to renegotiate communications exchanges, or to pursue them further to determine the precise meaning at a specific time. A phrase like "We must have lunch" may simply serve as a social lubricant, or it may, if pursued, be a genuine offer. If lunch is the desired outcome, then a response like "Right—let's check our calendars" may be appropriate. What Walter Truett Anderson calls the socially constructed reality of communication shifts under our feet, and we cannot automatically count on it to mean the same thing every time.[2] Problems of interpretation are compounded when the exchange is mediated through e-mail or answering machine messages, or video teleconferencing.

Things have changed a lot since the early eighties, when video teleconferencing rooms cost up to $750,000 to equip, not to mention the considerable transmission charges involved. One early room was structurally isolated from other rooms in the building and designed so that no two walls were parallel to each other in order to get high-quality audio. (In fact, getting the audio right has always been harder than getting the visual transmission right.)

Modular units and cookie-cutter room designs have lowered the costs of installing permanent video rooms. Meanwhile, rollabout units have made permanent equipment unnecessary. Given the high cost of office real estate and the shortage of conference rooms in most organizations, the rollabouts were a big hit as soon as they passed the minimum-quality threshold. By the early nineties, transportable rooms rolling down the corporate halls had replaced permanently installed rooms. Meanwhile, desktop video already offers both video telephoning and video conferencing without participants having to go to a special transmission location. Although the details and the costs are still uncertain, this capability will move the video conference into the home or anytime/anyplace office in the very near future.

Future video teleconferencing systems will build from research at Bell Communications Research, the University of Arizona, and Keio University, where the goal is to simulate being across a table or room from others who were actually at remote sites.[3] Novel camera and lens work allows a visual sense of reality that moves beyond simply seeing others over television monitors or projection screens.

Meeting support software turned a major corner in 1990, when IBM began commercially testing software developed by Jay Nunamaker and his team at the University of Arizona. The Arizona software (licensed to IBM by Ventana Corporation in Tucson) was the first meeting room software that normal business people with no special training could use with the help of a competent aide or facilitator. Software to support business meetings even without a special aide present is gradually entering the marketplace.

With the increased use of teams in business, the number of meetings is also going up—along with the frustrations inherent in meetings. Meeting support systems are currently geared toward providing technology and facilitation support for face-to-face meetings, although both providers and users expect links to meetings at a distance to become more common. The major problem is that the trained aides are needed to run the software. Public rooms are now available in various parts of the world, with a variety of electronic support tools with and without facilitation services.

Electronically supported meetings not only solve pressing business problems but offer their own advantages. They seem to go faster and run more efficiently than face-to-face meetings. Participants are often more conscientious about details of meeting planning and conduct. Thus, meetings are better organized, with agendas made up in advance and so on. Even without support technology, of course, greater efficiency would result if these same principles for planning meetings were followed.

Getting a group together to consider more options and then make decisions more quickly can shorten the length of time it takes to bring a product or service to market.

One guiding hope of electronic support technology as well as other forms of groupware is that the technology will help managers make better business decisions, especially on controversial issues, since the support allows anonymity, which in turn encourages candor.

Electronic tools for brainstorming and activities that yield creative ideas make it possible for groups to consider more options before reaching a decision. Since, with the help of the software, everyone can "talk" at once, the group can generate more ideas in a shorter time. The probability of pulling out the best "nuggets" of ideas is greater. Voting and anonymity could also lead to more unity in decision making or adopting new ideas as well as easier identification of points of disagreement. Anonymity allows groups to consider ideas on their own merits instead of their origin. Shy participants are less inhibited about expressing themselves in this medium. It is more difficult for individuals to dominate an electronically supported meeting, although certainly the kind of people who always try to dominate meetings will find new ways of doing so in electronic environments.

Some electronic support technology allows tracking of tasks and coordination of activities and improves managers' ability to keep in touch with sites around the world. Many users report that having a written file of what was agreed on during a meeting is especially helpful.

In sum, experience has shown that electronic meetings tend to have better agenda setting, task specification, designation of to-do lists, and so on. Electronic tools encourage discipline and accelerate these processes. Many systems function like electronic checklists to remind people of good meeting practices. The software of electronic support technologies may be structured in such a way that the group leader has more control over what happens, and when.

Supported meetings with real people grow more complex with the addition of an electronic or video opening on a distant time, space, place, or information matrix, providing both multimedia communications and distributed computer support. This hybrid technology combines electronic group support with video teleconferencing.

In the late seventies we conducted a pilot evaluation of video teleconferencing for a group of engineers building a new manufacturing plant. The engineers were located at both the home office and the construction site, with an unpleasant journey between the two places. Video teleconferencing seemed the obvious answer to span the communications gap.

During face-to-face meetings among the engineers, however, we observed that they rarely looked at each other while they spoke, even when talking directly to each other. Instead they looked at the physical models of the new plant or engineering drawings or plans. These models were the medium they used to communicate. Seeing another engineer's flesh-and-blood body during a meeting was not only unnecessary; it was distracting. Without the models, the engineers had difficulty communicating at all.

Our research and experience over the past twenty years suggests that many people, not just engineers, prefer to communicate through or even within models, which provide continuity for those who share them. Without flexible models they have difficulty communicating, particularly with those not trained to work with the models. It would be a mistake to simulate electronically a face-to-face meeting for such people, especially since they do not want to look at one another anyway.

In some instances ultra high fidelity audio gives a sense of social presence and intimacy that may surpass video. Audio focuses the senses on sound and voice intonation, important for subtle tasks like detecting lying. Binaural sound gives the feeling of a virtual meeting table, with voices coming from appropriate spots around the table. If all the meeting participants have access to the same model through video or computer networks, the combined media can facilitate communication and assist in productive work.

Mike Noll and others at Bell Laboratories worked on "teleportation through communications" in the mid-seventies.[4] In this early vision, participants wore helmets, goggles, and earphones, all of which together contributed to a sense of "telepresence" from remote sites. This work anticipated increased bandwidth and reduced costs, which have now reached the point that teleportation through communications is practical, especially if the goal is to work within models rather than simulate face-to-face meetings.

Meeting within models is just one dramatic exploration of how work environments can be made to match the needs of particular teams more closely. A conducive setting that includes both physical and psychic space is vital for productive work, but what that setting is naturally varies from one organization to another. Developing a clear notion of the ideal collaborative environment is important.

One possible answer is the virtual reality world of Dr. Stella Hawkins, who when we visited her pulled up a new version of a molecular model in her headset display. She'd been waiting all week to get a look. An informal group of exchange scientists at the North Carolina research center had already attached their annotations. The virtual reality dimension enabled her to "go inside" the model (called "scientific visualization") and observe its formation and relationships.

As she prodded a node in the model, it pushed back just as its physical characteristics suggested it should.

"Note the change in external texture as the model moves toward entropy," she heard Grant Sears say in audio playback.

"He's right," Art Little added.

"I was wondering when you'd show up," Stella said to Art, whose office is on the West Coast.

The two scientists toured the model's interior structure. "What about the synergistic reaction?" she wondered aloud.

She and Art ran the program and added the label HEAT TRANSFER below the virtual model as it simulated the process of mixing with a cooler twin molecular model. They drew in the steam that would normally result from this interaction and moved on to the next stop in their tour of the model.

If a meeting "location" is inside a model like this, the actual geographical whereabouts of the participants are irrelevant; they can be anywhere the network can find them.

The fishnet organizational style will require such flexibility, with virtual meeting environments used as needed to "info-mediate" disparate teams. Of course, these opportunities must be balanced against issues of corporate boundaries, intellectual property, and security, which are likely to be sticky as electronic webs connect workers with various, and potentially competing, affiliations and loyalties.

Meetings within models also provide an indirect aid to cross-cultural communication among the members of global teams. Models provide a shared frame of reference for people from different cultural backgrounds. Visual imagery bridges barriers across differences of language and customs. Meeting inside a model could logically connect communications protocols to the model itself rather than the cultural norms of a geographical area. A model creates its own culture and serves as common ground.

Scientists, engineers, designers, architects, and others in model-oriented professions often find it difficult to share their work and their ways of thinking with others. Time spent communicating with managers is one of the major bottlenecks in developing new product prototypes and packaging. If a team could bring a manager into its virtual world, the review process would shorten dramatically.

Some managers come away from virtual reality demonstrations with unhealthy visions of holograms dancing in their heads. The hype of the virtual reality movement obscures the practical potential for re-thinking basic ways in which people interact with computers. Brenda Laurel, one of the leaders in the field of virtual reality, made this case in her address to the first annual Virtual Reality Conference in 1990: "We have to stop putting our pedal to the floor on [video] resolution and emphasize ambiguity and incomplete sensory information."[5] In fact, what is technically incomplete or ambiguous may be most useful to the end user. Meetings within models can have three-dimensional graphics, animation, and high-quality audio. Scott Fisher, formerly of NASA and one of the leading researchers in the field, describes this not-quite-real virtual state as "a cross between a cartoon and a dream."[6] That's good enough for most people, who would be much more productive if they could communicate through models consider-ably cruder than 3-D holography.

The idea of meetings within models stimulates rethinking how we interact with computers. It is appropriate, for instance, to think about human-computer interactions as theater. Just as a playwright designs an experience for an audience, so software designers create an experi-ence for users, and in the case of virtual reality, the audience are also actors on the software stage. Brenda Laurel, for instance, has a doctor-ate in theater and is the author of a book called *Computers as Theater.*[7]

The idea of meeting in models is related to that of team rooms, a no-tion that is gradually catching on in businesses. Today's team rooms may be equipped in various ways, but the important characteristic is that the room takes on the identity of the team. Wall charts, displays, models, data, and other artifacts that are meaningful to the team are left there. When team members enter the room they are instantly re-minded of the history and goals of the team. The room becomes a kind of clubhouse. Combined with virtual reality capabilities, the team can design its own ideal collaborative work space without the constraints of physical reality.

Telecommunications and computing systems should function like information utilities, with tools that meet the teams' immediate needs while providing a common environment for exchange across the entire enterprise. Within large companies the need for in-house, highly spe-cialized computer expertise is waning. The priesthood of central com-puting has already given way to a secular world of laypeople playing with multiplying microprocessors.

Bigger changes are coming from even smaller computers, some-times called "information appliances." Just a few years ago, infor-mation systems organizations concentrated on "maintaining a clean database" in their central mainframe computers. Network structures and powerful small appliances allow data and computer resources to scatter throughout an enterprise. Data are now distributed across organizations and even across companies. It is still important to keep this data "clean," but the means of doing so have changed dramatically. Technical skills used to be most important for data hygiene; today, organizational skills are more important.

Outsourcing both network maintenance and applications development will become increasingly common. The role of chief information officer will disappear or be radically revised. As Max Hopper sees the future, "a company trumpeting the appointment of a new chief information officer will seem as anachronistic as a company today naming a new vice president for water and gas."[8]

Decentralized "nontechnical" staff who learn just enough (and learn it just in time) to develop the applications they need at the time they need them will be key users of computers. End users have already developed many applications. They may need coaching and support from a central information systems organization, but such organizations will be relatively unimportant.

This evolution parallels what occurred with centralized strategic planning, which over the past decade has given way to distributed planning, often as part of line business activities. Just as planning became too important to leave to planners, information systems are too important to leave to a separate information system's internal organization.

Meanwhile the availability and ease of access to outside information is increasing exponentially. In such an environment, skill in what our colleague Paul Saffo calls information surfing—negotiating, filtering and assessing information, condensing and coalescing it into significant, manageable packages, and conveying it to the right person or persons—is far more important than hearty good cheer or micromanagerial aptitude.

The anytime/anyplace work world is upon us, particularly in functional areas like sales. Good salespeople spend most of their time out with customers. For them, ultralight pen-based laptops, cellular modems, information appliances of all shapes and functions, shared filing, and plain-paper fax machines that can function as remote printers and photocopiers are a few examples of the many devices for infomediation that can keep them in touch with the home office and maintain their sense of continuity in the global economy. At the same time, coping with the complexity of cultural rules presents a real challenge.

It depends on human skills, resourcefulness, and flexibility not easily enhanced by technology.

Common sense tells us that subtle communications should be saved for face-to-face meetings while routine exchanges can occur over electronic surrogates. This is the essence of the Japanese concept of *haragei*, which is defined as the art of communicating through the stomach, or *hara*. Michihiro Matsomuto explains, "A man who uses *haragei* says one thing and quite another and means both. . . . One of my stock definitions of *haragei* is the art of influencing others on the strength of one's personality or self-effacing acts rather than on the validity of his agreements."[9]

This art has more to do with ritual silences between words than it does with the words themselves. It is a concept that is strange to most Americans. If a global team is made up of Americans and Japanese, cross-cultural understanding is vital, especially for close anticipatory teamwork.

The answer lies in both cultural knowledge and some form of *haragei*, developed or at least maintained via electronic media. Given the physical distance between the United States and Japan, the use of electronic media is mandatory. With it, intimacy among global team members becomes possible.

19

Rewarding Work

Even after intimacy develops among team members through electronic mediation, the problem of how to reward teams remains. At the moment few organizations have comprehensive policies or programs of team rewards in place.

But there are organizations with partial programs, or with divisions or departments struggling to find ways to compensate and encourage teamwork and reduce the emphasis on individual achievement over group effort. These small efforts offer vague outlines of the shape team rewards could take in the future. Such rewards will shift dramatically from a focus on what used to be called the competitive edge to what we can call the cooperative edge.

Cooperation depends on clear, accurate communication. Before they can be rewarded—before they can even succeed—members of global teams must understand one another despite linguistic and cultural differences. The great anthropologist E. T. Hall has said that culture is communication, and communication is culture. In his classic book *The Silent Language* he propounded a broad and deep notion of communication, with an emphasis on the important role of the "out-of-awareness" side. "It will be helpful if the reader thinks of culture as analogous to music," Hall wrote. "If a person hasn't heard music, it is impossible to describe. Before the days of written scores, people learned informally by imitation. Man was able to exploit the potential of music only when he started writing musical scores. This is what must be done for culture."[1]

People working in cross-cultural organizations play the new music of cross-cultural work, which in the foreseeable future will be something like improvisational jazz, with some general agreement about rhythm and chord progressions but lots of room for individual creativity. Such improvisational cooperation involves an increasing reliance on self-management. As decision-making power moves away from the center, the grip of the home office loosens. This means organizations must continue to set norms and create a corporate culture but not lay down rigid rules.

The exact ways in which companies combine global and local elements will vary. Without a scorecard, it is already difficult to tell competitors from collaborators. Some large companies are in so many business areas now that almost everyone is a competitor in some sense. At the same time, competitors at one point in the distribution chain can be suppliers or customers at another.

Traditional rewards for work are material: promotions with increased pay, bonuses, stock options, and generous benefit packages. In the team-based fishnet structure, particularly those with a global perspective, it is important to think creatively about alternative kinds of rewards, which might include free child care, stock options for all employees, benefits for gay and lesbian partners, tuition subsidies for employees with children in college, tutoring for school-age children, free income tax preparation, vacation for newlyweds, family leave, stipends for getting a college degree, or full unlimited sick pay.[2] Such systems can apply to successful teams as easily as to individuals.

Of course, job security used to be a high-priority nonmaterial benefit. But fewer and fewer companies promote from within, or acknowledge what Procter and Gamble's mission statement continues to regard as "the vital importance of continuing employment" within the same corporation. Just as material rewards are disappearing, job security is barely a memory and company loyalty a psychic fossil. Without security, company loyalty disappears as well.

Job security will depend on being prepared for the next team assignment when the call is sent out. Those who perform well have the security of knowing they are likely to be called again. Predictable stairing up a corporate hierarchy grows increasingly uncommon, and frequent movement around the webs of organizational activity is increasing. This movement is very often across corporate borders, where security depends on personal networks and loyalty means attachment and commitment to colleagues in the fuzzy fishnet structure, whatever their company affiliation.

Organizations struggling to retain employee loyalty without offering security haven't learned the rewards lesson. It's a new world out there. "What," the CEO of a rapidly downsizing corporation asked recently, "can we do to increase loyalty—especially now, when we have to limit our long-term commitments to employees?"

This is the wrong question. Routine attempts to increase employee loyalty, especially in a time of such flux, are fruitless or counterproductive. It is simply not possible to demand what you cannot command. Loyalty to whom, or to what? Corporate loyalty has little currency in the interlinked economy, when today's employer may move, die out, or change its spots. In the fishnet organization, the "collegial network of shared values," as Kenichi Ohmae calls it, loyalty is an ever-shifting locus, based on those shared values.[3] Loyalty is collegial, not corporate.

This means that selfish competition, between employees as between corporations, is the road to ruin. The interlinked economy leaves little room for bullies.

As companies extend themselves across borders, hire locally, form alliances with complementary organizations in other places for mutual benefit, and shift their emphasis from maximizing profits to serving customers, the need for cooperation increases. The growth of the fishnet enterprise will demand the ability to cross cultures easily. Self-benefiting cooperation that offers advantages to all participants will be an essential personal and organizational skill. Individuals with the cooperative edge will gain greatly.

In the thoroughly interlinked economy, the fishnet organization is driven by teams, which are an effective and flexible way of organizing for short-lived projects. Most people like to participate in them, finding them exciting and rewarding. But rewards must become more team oriented as well. Cooperative enterprise is not powered by individual reward, nor does it thrive on single-minded loyalty to an isolated corporate logo.

Since corporations can no longer demand or offer loyalty, corporate loyalty cannot motivate people. So what will motivate them?

Rosabeth Moss Kanter has identified some important motives in her groundbreaking article "The New Managerial Work": mission (giving people something they can believe in), agenda control (giving people a say in what happens), sharing in value creation (immediate or delayed financial rewards as well as awards and public recognition), learning (new skills development), and reputation (opportunities to enhance one's own reputation). She concludes that the new security is not employment security but *employability* security, employees' confidence that if they are laid off they will be able to find jobs with other companies.[4]

For example, when 3Com had a downturn in its business in Silicon Valley, there were layoffs. All employees who were laid off were immediately picked up by other companies. This experience caused the corporation to realize that it could not promise employees lifelong employment, but it *could* promise employability. It now has a strong policy of employability, rather than the traditional job security model.

The nineties version of corporate loyalty like that at 3Com is still unusual. But long-term employability may be as good as or better than long-term employment with a single corporation for both employer and employee, since it gives them a wider range of options. When 3Com built a new corporate headquarters in Santa Clara, it also adopted a policy that it will not grow by casually adding buildings or people. Instead it will maintain a strong core staff in different areas of competency to build local area networks and at the same time will develop long-term contractual relationships for other staff roles. (See Figure 19-1.)

When asked what he would like to leave behind as his legacy at General Electric, CEO Jack Welch replied, "a company that's able to change at least as fast as the world is changing, and people whose real income is secure because they're winning and whose psychic income is rising because every person is participating."[5]

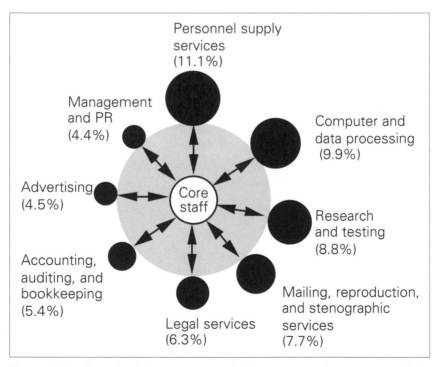

Figure 19-1 Growth of the outsource web (percent annual average growth in U.S. labor force in the 1980s)

This notion of psychic income is compelling. Once a threshold level of income is assured and such necessities as health care are no longer at issue, the intangible rewards of satisfaction, excitement, pleasure, community, and achievement are, it turns out, more important than material rewards. Reporting on a recent poll on the subject of rewards by Chicago consultants Kuczmarski and Associates, Joan Rigdon has noted in *The Wall Street Journal* that "new product development teams at 77 Fortune 500 companies rated a sense of accomplishment as the No. 1 factor that motivates them. Peer recognition ranked second. In descending order, the next highest motivators were visibility to top management, career advancement, compensation, and peer pressure."[6] The findings of this poll are supported by the National Opinion Research Center's General Social Survey rankings, which have identified the top five factors as interesting, useful work; income; advancement opportunities; job security; and time off.[7]

At the bottom of the list in the Kuczmarski survey, the carrot of compensation and the stick of peer pressure were weak energizers indeed. The top two items, a sense of accomplishment and peer recognition, are both intangible psychic rewards.

A recent national survey by the Families and Work Institute provides still more insight into employees' priorities. The results indicate that economic rewards are far less important than many people believed: "The top five reasons for taking jobs were open communications, effect of the job on personal and family life, nature of the work, management quality, and supervisor characteristics. These factors, interestingly, all have to do with the quality of the work environment. In contrast, only 35 percent of the workers rated salary/wage as a very important reason for joining their current employer."[8]

Businesses are just waking up to what educators and parents have known for generations: that pride in what one does is the most powerful of all rewards. With materialism everywhere in decline, in part because it has failed to provide the satisfactions people really need, true rewards have room to grow into the light.

But while participation on business teams can offer enormous psychic satisfactions, it can also cause great distress. People ask themselves why they should volunteer for high-pressure teams when only individual performance will be rewarded. The answer is that they have no choice. Teams are here to stay, and participating in them is the only option. Workers' distress can be reduced by adequate and effective reward systems and attention to maintaining a cooperative team spirit.

In the past, star performers were often rewarded by promotions into management jobs, where they sometimes flourished but often did not. Some people do not make good managers, or do not care for management tasks. Instead of promotions, companies must find ways of rewarding employees with whatever is important to them as individuals. For their part, employees must communicate effectively what they want and need. The ultimate responsibility for determining rewards falls back on those who receive them.

Those who succeed in the global economy will follow Socrates' advice: "Know thyself." They will know who they are and what motivates them. Business organizations can no longer run their employees' lives; the old-style paternalistic multinational corporation has collapsed in the wreckage of the industrial era, taking traditional ideas of "headquarters," of "overseas," of "us-versus-them" with it. Serving a company in a foreign land, for example, is no longer either a privilege or a hardship. It is a fact of life in the new world. Teams cross corporate, gender, age, and national lines. Rewards must be tailored to the context and culture of individuals, and only those individuals can say for sure what their rewards should be. The challenge of finding appropriate rewards to keep employees and contractors involved, interested, and happy comes down to the connection between individual managers and workers.

The approach taken by 3Com to the problem of rewards is novel: the company puts the responsibility in other hands. For instance, the telephones at 3Com are answered by people who work for an outside contractor. They are not temps, however, but long-term employees of the contracting company, which employs telephone receptionists and other clerical workers in career path roles, and contracts these services permanently to companies like 3Com. The contractor is a strong presence at 3Com headquarters, but it is a separate organization, offering promotions and rewards independently of the client. Rewards are thus brought closer to the line employee.

At the same time, 3Com has its own employees in jobs in the core areas of its business. As one 3Com manager told us, "We know a lot about network engineering, but we don't know about answering telephones. Why not hire some company that's good at that, the way we're good at global data networks?"

The appearance of these "insiders from the outside" on the organizational scene creates delicate issues. Do you invite these workers to office parties? Do you treat them like full-time employees on a day-to-day basis? Probably, but the new work protocol can be tricky.

Another approach to rewards is that of George Radcliffe's clothing company, which organized pairs of teams, called "families," to solve specific problems in reengineering the horizontal flow of the business from supplier to customer. Eighty percent of the teams' evaluations are based on each family's achievement of goals. Cooperation therefore rewards everyone.

But though there are pockets within major corporations where some form of team incentive and reward is in place, such efforts are unusual. Lynda Applegate found only a few scattered examples of businesses that have completed the transition toward self-managing teams and team rewards. GE Canada is one. The transition process involved employees and management at all levels. On average, it took twenty-four to thirty months for the self-managing teams to come into existence, from announcement of their formation to full operation. A twenty-five-year employee said of the process of shifting toward teams and team rewards, "We never expected that it would take so long and be such an agonizing process."[9]

The transition took place through a series of internal meetings and exchanges. All teams were responsible for developing their own approach to self-management; there were no standard procedures. Peer evaluation within the teams has become the norm. This means the entire evaluation process for each team member now takes as much as four weeks, but employees report that they get much better feedback than before. The teams do not make specific salary and grade level recommendations, but the peer evaluations are important input to the co ordinators who do make these decisions. In short, the experience at GE Canada has been a good one, but it has also been a slow and often taxing transition. This approach to team rewards is one possible solution, but not an easy one.

AT&T Capital, a division of AT&T, is another example of a company that has shown an awareness of alternative rewards in its reengineering program. Teams and hierarchies evaluate each worker (referred to as an "organization member" rather than an "employee") according to specific job areas. As one analyst of the new organization observed, "The result unhooked rewards from hierarchy. . . . An organization member's pay was tied to the market for his or her specific skills, and internal equity became a consideration only within the person's job family. Former links to rank and status were almost completely eliminated. Moreover, this bigger emphasis on variable pay allowed individuals or teams to be rewarded for performance."[10]

AT&T Capital's reorganized structure is still characterized by the inherent hierarchies of the parent company, which remains the traditional center. However, reengineering has allowed flatter team-oriented structures to govern the corporation's day-to-day business and its rewards for performance. This is innovation at the edges of the emerging fishnet. AT&T, even after the layoffs of the last ten years, is so large that it encompasses in its different divisions both positive and negative outcomes of reengineering programs.

Another successful example in the constantly metamorphosing, interlinked information economy is Rosenbluth Travel's electronic net, built on existing airline reservations systems (American Airlines' SABRE systems and United's Apollo). The corporation provides travel agents with specialized services that can be configured according to the needs of the marketplace or the customer.

The members of the Rosenbluth International Alliance serve one another's travel customers, making cross-referrals as appropriate. The employees of alliance member firms are carefully screened to ensure that they have personal qualities that are compatible with the Rosenbluth approach to customers. Alliance members are given incentives to participate fully in the international cooperative network: for example, each member has one vote, regardless of its size, and it shares costs of the alliance in proportion to sales. This global structure has had a very successful beginning, and it will be interesting to see how it develops over time.

The development of team reward systems appropriate for North American businesses will not be easy. In Japan, where teams have been a way of life for years, the culture is more collective than that of the highly individualistic United States, and the Japanese model will never play in the United States. Companies in Nordic countries offer better models for a system of team rewards in U.S. corporations. Telia, Sweden's newly privatized telecommunications provider, Volvo, and SAS tend to fall between the extremes of American and Japanese companies in their programs to encourage team cooperation.

One example of a program to reward team initiative in a U.S. company is that of American Express, which began its Chairman's Award for Quality program in 1990 to recognize and reward employee teams that had identified opportunities to improve quality and organized themselves to find solutions. Nearly five hundred teams took part in the competition during the first year, resulting in a wide range of innovations. Seven of those teams, one from each business unit, received the chairman's award and were honored at a luncheon in New York City. Such programs to reward both temporary and permanent work teams are likely to grow in popularity.

Milliken and Company, a recent Malcolm Baldridge National Quality Award winner, recognizes both individuals and teams in a highly visible process that is perceived as a major motivator by employees. Team rewards include participation in training for new skills development, a variety of awards and other forms of public recognition, and the chance to work closely with senior executives.

As cultures both national and corporate mix and clash, sharing experiences across companies, industries, and nations will be necessary. Because incentives and rewards are culturally linked, cross-fertilization should yield creative ideas. Loyalty in the emerging business organization, which will be personal and communal, will be satisfying in its own right. Those who participate in teams will find that the Rolodex is their most effective tool in maintaining employability security from project to project. Rewards will go to teams and team members who maintain a cooperative edge.

20

Learning

on the Fly

Roger Simpson, a sixteen-year veteran mechanic with a major airline, always prided himself on his knowledge and skill servicing the systems that ran the Boeing 737, but on a bitter night in January at Chicago's O'Hare Airport, he wants to call it quits.

He's used to the cold and the wind driving icy sleet across the tarmac. It isn't the weather that bothers him; it's the service support system for the new aircraft. He feels like a fool in his virtual reality goggles as he trudges through the driving rain to the parked aircraft. He has only the most general knowledge of the new plane's systems, which are more complex and intricate than any he has ever seen. The pilot reported that an intermittent failure light was flashing, indicating a problem with the left cargo door, and Roger is anxious about whether he can fix the problem.

The plane is due to leave in forty minutes. A late or canceled flight means thousands of dollars in lost revenues.

"How hard can it be?" he mutters.

A voice in his right ear says, "What's that?"

"Oh, nothing." Roger taps his fingers in the icy air in front of his chin, feeling for the microphone that isn't there. "Uh, this is Simpson. Radio check," he mumbles uncomfortably. The induction device attached to the tiny earphone picks up his words from the bone near his ear. Roger forgot that there is no microphone.

"How do you read, Roger?"

"It's OK, Irv. I hear you fine."

"Good. How is it out there?"

"Horrible. I'm in the cargo hold now."

"OK. Let me know what you find."

"Will do."

Roger touches a key and talks, first asking for a schematic of the fiber-optic network operating the cargo door. He works cautiously but accurately.

Twenty minutes later he reports that the problem was a faulty light.

"So," Irv says, "did you learn anything?" Irv always asks that when Roger services an airplane. And Roger always says, "Yes, Irv. I learned something." He usually does learn something, but it annoys him that Irv always asks the question. And if Roger doesn't say yes, Irv always has a long chain of follow-up questions to find out what could have been done better. Roger is getting a headache.

Irv isn't human. He is an intelligent knowledge base with control over a stable of agents, all built into the airline's information system. He's named after a former master mechanic who took early retirement six months ago.

Trudging back to the maintenance office through the sleet, Roger realizes that in fact he does like the new system. He doesn't need to learn something in detail until he actually needs to use the information. It's always new, and it's usually useful. But Roger misses the real Irv, just as he misses working on the 737. He knew that plane inside and out.

Workers like Roger in the new business culture will need both to be willing to learn new material on the spot and to have access to necessary information at the right time. Sometimes this learning is continual, as in Roger's case. At other times it may be crash learning for a specific project.

Boeing already offers what has come to be called "performance support" to service its new aircraft. The systems, developed from computer-based training and emerging multimedia capabilities, provide information and training for specific procedures in the workplace itself so that relative novices can carry out the required tasks effectively. Typical applications are customer service and field maintenance support. Providing support to field staff working alone is particularly important.

With delivery of the 777 aircraft, Boeing is including on-line training with personal computers and special software. The system provides mechanics like Roger the information they need where and when they need it, even while crawling in the cargo hold at night (using a "heads-up" virtual reality display that the mechanic wears like eyeglasses). For the 777, a resource for continual learning is part of the product, and the creation and maintenance of that resource is the responsibility of the manufacturer. Performance support offers just-in-time learning as needed. It includes quick searches, with recall in visual and quantitative form, comparing the reality in the field with the learning resources available electronically.

The world, its culture, and its technologies are changing too rapidly for managers to depend on what they learned in the past. Learning must be on time, in time, just in time, every time. Organizations and individuals need to create an environment in which they can continually renew their knowledge.

Three-dimensional graphics products for use in engineering design are now practical. Boeing's 777 is the closest thing yet to a paperless airplane; virtual models of the aircraft were produced on Silicon Graphics workstations. As one writer reports, "Boeing is striving for 100% digital definition of the 777, thus reducing or eliminating hand drawings, major mockups, and master models. Some 2,000 computer terminals using the CATIS three-dimensional display system will provide the backbone for this effort and make possible the major implementation of the design/build concept."[1] Such efforts make Boeing a leading practitioner of virtual reality techniques, even though the term *virtual reality* is rarely used in the company's executive offices. (In the business world, it is wise to use such terms only among consenting adults.) This is info-mediation applied to practical needs for equipment servicing in the field.

The new work environment includes unique learning requirements that classroom training alone cannot meet. Just-in-time learning moves ever closer to performance itself. Training cannot simply prepare people to perform in the future; it must support their performance in the present.

A variant of just-in-time learning is to incorporate specialized knowledge that the user doesn't have in a software tool so that with the tool the user can handle tasks successfully. An example is Macin-Tax, for income tax preparation, which explains to the user why he must do certain things, what exactly he needs to do and in what order, and where to get more information. Other examples are software for redesigning kitchens or adding decks onto houses. These tools, which teach through "dialogues" with the user, include a knowledge base the user can interrogate. The starting point for developing such tools, of course, is a thorough understanding of how the tasks in question should be carried out.

Another approach to just-in-time learning evolved from expert systems but is based on the cumulative knowledge of a team rather than on that of a single expert. Collaborative just-in-time learning includes what employees currently doing the job know, and it thus builds up over time an increasingly useful knowledge base that is then available to other team members as needed. So far the best examples are knowledge-based products aimed at the teams handling questions at a help desk, but the same approach can be used to build organizational memory for any job or activity. Collaborative learning is especially applicable in situations where it can help a work group avoid remaking old mistakes. In education, it allows individual students to contribute to the knowledge base directly, as "authors." Such systems are based on the assumption that human beings learn best when they have taken part in discovering information and ideas themselves.

Learning is more effective as a social, not an individual, endeavor. Work at the Institute for Research on Learning in Palo Alto, California, started from the hunch that people learn less through formal instruction than through social interaction. The institute's subsequent research indicates that people learn more swiftly when they belong to "overlapping communities of practice," or groups with differing specialties. In this way learning gradually returns to the part of the workplace where it is used, and is no longer a specialized offering of training departments.

Workers need more knowledge than they have time to acquire, so it's important for organizations to provide information and insights where and when needed. If they don't have the skills that departed employees took with them, many confront constant uncertainty.

Furthermore, the organization must keep learning resources fresh. Static information is soon out of date. Knowledge must be flexible to have value. Until recently, training tended to be a package of specific information about what was known at a single point in time, like a snapshot. Training *is* a form of learning, but workers in the information era need more than snapshots; they need the learning equivalent of motion pictures, continually updated and made easily accessible as they work.

Learning is enhanced by technologies that help people understand difficult information. Instead of tables of numbers, computer-based graphics can give instantly recognizable representations of complex relationships. Depictions of dynamic processes can show change visually over time as well as multiple factors interacting with one another.

Current learning applications are predominantly for pilot or military training, but spinoffs are appearing in entertainment products such as games and amusement park rides. SimLife, a computer toy from Maxis Corporation, simulates a world in which species evolve and struggle for survival. The user plays God, setting the terrain, access to nutrition, even the genetic makeup of the creatures in the world. Similar simulations, based on the work of the Santa Fe Institute on artificial life, complexity theory, and emergent systems, might model the world economy in a highly realistic way.

Simulations can provide the best training for real-world challenges, and advances in technology now enable users to learn from extremely convincing experiences. Some of these experiences even result in momentary confusion between the simulation and reality. They can promote understanding of complex models and theories.

Gloria Gery describes a customer service system being developed by American Express that trains novices to perform like experts. It integrates multimedia data, information, training, and tiered coaching and prompting. The agent using the system can provide customers with greatly improved service since information about the individual customer and options for response are available immediately.

Now that people are accustomed to video and computer technology, increasingly they may want learning and training to be more like MTV, channel surfing, or their other computer-based work. It is not enough merely to speed up the process, however. The speed of just-in-time learning is less than worthless if the information itself is wrong.

The notion of core competencies provides a useful perspective from which to view organizations and learning. Core competencies, "the collective learning in the organization, especially how to coordinate diverse production skills and integrate multiple streams of technologies,"[2] are likely to be the nodes on the organizational fishnet that most express a company's strengths. Through analyzing these competencies, businesses can discover the most important principles that should guide organizational change and development through uncertain periods. The most important competencies, however, may be at the edge of the formal organization, not at the core.

Rosenbluth Travel adopted a learning approach to the complex business climate after airline deregulation, but it also kept a focus on its traditional competencies: customer relations and service. It did not increase the use of information networks for the sake of being technologically advanced but rather in order to build on its travel services and make them more attractive to corporate clients.

The chance to learn valuable new skills will replace some of the ties that bound employees to their organizations in the past. The company that provides adequate opportunities for new learning will nurture employability security and loyalty. Some companies have already instituted company-wide universities and incentives for learning. Just-in-time learning includes life skills such as English usage and communications, as well as training in using specific tools, but in the future it will embrace a far broader range of subject matter presented according to varied methodologies.

One successful executive told us that he needs to "repot" himself every few years, to put down new roots, to expand and become broader as he gets older. A number of dispossessed managers are finding that the restructuring frenzy of the past decade has created initially unwelcome but ultimately fruitful opportunities for such growth. Though exposing the old roots may be painful, especially if you're root bound, the greater freedom to develop in a larger pot is invigorating.

Jim Parker lost his job as a senior financial officer for a pathologically downsizing company in 1989. For a couple of years he scratched out a living, feeling sorry for himself and dissipating his savings. He and his wife had always wanted to live in the country, so one day they sold their house and moved. After all, no particular reason kept them in the city; there was no work anyway.

Over the next two years Jim found that he had transplanted himself in what certainly felt like a larger container, one that gave him room to grow. In the process he created a novel entrepreneurial profession for himself, offering his services on a temporary basis to companies just starting up in biological and medical technology. "I work two or three days a week, get the company going, take stock options, and move on when the company has either proved itself viable or withered away."

He has, in addition, hatched his own solution to the challenge of balancing love and work. He finds he must be vigilant in maintaining a clear boundary between them. Although he commutes up to three hours on workdays, he does so by choice. He can live where he wants to live, and the commuting time offers a restful transition between the different intensity levels of office and home. Once he got over the shock of repotting, Jim found that he could develop in new directions. Working like this at serial start-ups, and thus having a chain of varying jobs, has made his life easier.

Realizing that his former way of life when he worked for the corporation was destructive to his family, he is now rigorous about protecting the new life he has made. "It seemed I was always at work when my son needed me. He ended up on the street. Then I lost my corporate job. It was a terrible time, but we bailed him out and got our lives back together. I wouldn't go back to that life for anything now."

Jim makes it a point to arrive at his office at the client company at eight-thirty, and to leave at exactly five in the afternoon. Every day he gives a full day's work, but no more. This is a nonnegotiable point, one he is in a position to enforce. "When I'm not at the office, I'm not working, period. Time out of the office is my time."

In fact, he has no permanent office of his own, no business phone or fax or computer. He carries no business cards other than the ones his companies give him. And he loves every minute of it. "Have MBA," he says, "will travel." He is a CFO for hire.

Henry Grossman was a high-level middle manager in his forties at a well-known computer company that does research in Silicon Valley. In the turmoil of the early nineties, Henry discovered that he couldn't justify his own slot on the organizational chart, so he more or less voluntarily joined the flood of recently unemployed middle managers in that summer's round of layoffs.

After the initial shock brought by his rather sudden decision had worn away, Henry says, he felt mostly relief. Seated in a coffee shop in Palo Alto, he shakes his head. "It was time to leave," he says. "I'd been there ten years, and before that I'd been ten years with a research institute. Looking back, I realize I should have left both places earlier than I did."

Now he is looking around for a new challenge, the next big wave. He smiles when he talks about his layoff. "The fact is," he admits, "I fired myself. I could have tried harder to find another place in the company. I probably would have succeeded. But I didn't want to make a slot in the org chart. That wasn't what I was, anyway."

So what was he?

"I was a node in a network. Most of what I did, the real work, was building alliances, coalitions, informal relationships to get things done. None of these things showed up on the chart. So I was out. Fortunately."

Henry now works part-time with a firm he had formerly hired as consultants. His previous employer is one of his clients: since Henry's organizational memory walked out the door with him, now his former employer wants to buy it back in consulting time, by the hour. Perhaps both are better off: the corporation appreciates Henry's skills more, and Henry has greater freedom to pursue his own interests. Though he lost his job, he regained control of his life.

Catherine and Roger, a two-income couple laid off from Henry's company, where she had been a senior researcher in the R&D department and he a programmer and engineer, moved from the West Coast to the Southeast. Both took their job loss as an opportunity. Catherine had always wanted to try to write, and Roger wanted to become more involved in massage and physical therapy. Now they live in North

Carolina, where Roger has clients for both his programming skills and his physical therapy business. They took their generous severance packages to incubate an entirely different lifestyle.

Not everyone has this kind of opportunity, of course, but Catherine and Roger's story illustrates the potential for individuals to restructure their priorities, if they are able to envision the possibilities in the midst of the pain of layoffs. These new North Carolinians are a strong couple who both weathered their layoffs to take their lives in new directions and their relationship to a new level.

A final example: George Radcliffe's company was not in financial trouble when it decided to reengineer; sales were good, the cash flow positive, brand recognition high. The company had an excellent reputation. Management felt this was the perfect time to rethink the business, when there was no crisis. In this sense, George's company was one of the fortunate ones.

But the human content of organizations, like business content, changes with reengineering. Roles change along with functions. Leaders are either recast or cast away.

George, an engaging, family-centered man, cheerfully acknowledges that he is a holdover from a past age, an Organization Man who survived the post-organization crash. He is loyal to the company that has employed him for all of his working life because of the opportunities it has given him to achieve greater affluence than his parents, and he is grateful that the company has not let him down. His life, however, is forever changed.

The "repotted" George lost his airy office with the view and the original artworks on its opulent walls. Now, in the maze of cubicles that used to be closed offices, groups constantly mingle and their ideas cross-fertilize. Energy is high, though everyone is still feeling the way in the new work world.

The intent in reengineering at the company was to completely redesign not only the way work was done but also to think about how work was done. This has meant that George has had to consider very hard what his skills really are.

He admits that it is the hardest thing he has ever done. He knew how to do his old job, but that job is no longer there. Like everyone else, he's starting over. At least in his case, the boundary between love and work remains after reengineering. But, he adds, "It was terrible in the beginning. All of my old habits, the way I understood the structure of my business, were in the way. I was constantly trying to understand and adjust my relationships with team members, people who had been my bosses and my employees before. I was very unsure for a long time, even with vendors and customers.

"Now, though, it's like dancing. I feel like I can move more freely, constantly moving with my partners, changing my role as needed. It's kind of fun."

Whatever the circumstances, repotting means learning new skills, taking new directions, having more room to grow. In the new millennium products will appear and disappear as fast as technological changes make them possible, and all workers without exception will be forced to adapt, learn, re-adapt and learn again. Repotting will be a normal part of life, and through it a new way of working with others will emerge.

The issues of performance support and needs for repotting suggest that new information systems must evolve to make learning available when and where it is needed. The Answer Garden, for example, an important research system for collaborative learning developed at MIT, is designed around an organic metaphor. The system allows organizations to develop databases of commonly asked questions, which grow as new questions arise and are answered in a way similar to the development of files of frequently asked questions, or FAQs, that have popped up all over the Internet to help newcomers navigate.[3]

The metaphor of reengineering, with its mechanical, deterministic resonance, lures us into thinking that the processes of memory and continuity can be automated. It is therefore surely significant that researchers at MIT, the mecca of engineering and mechanical design, have used the metaphor of a garden to describe their system of organizational memory and collaborative learning. If MIT can't automate it, nobody can.

Cultivation in this garden is a more potent metaphor, suggesting an organic nurturing process, unlike more mechanical terms like *input* or *download.* Looking across the complex areas of communications, continuity, and culture, it is obvious that the organization of the nineties must be prepared to "grow" itself. Its performance depends on careful cultivation.

A vivid example of this combination of learning and performance is Electronic Campus, which grew out of research at Apple Computer. The developers asked themselves what was at the time a radical question: "What would be the impact on competency and competency building if we supported learning in the work environment, rather than thinking of learning and working as separated in time, place and structure?"[4] When Apple began a round of layoffs, Electronic Campus grew into a powerful "knowledge garden" for the human resources department that helps people repot themselves.

Electronic Campus (which grew from a system called NNABLE) was first developed for Apple technical coordinators (ATCs), the people who troubleshoot when users within Apple have problems with their computers. These workers had an important base of experience and would call on each other informally when they needed help. NNABLE sought to cultivate and expand this interpersonal knowledge network instead of replacing it. Working together as a team, systems designers and the ATCs began by studying how ATCs get to be good at what they do. Then they planned the system to support that process and improve on it through a series of focus groups, interviews, and field studies. ATCs were even asked to record their stories into tape recorders as they worked, for later analysis of patterns of response.

NNABLE suggested options and documented what was learned during each ATC's problem-solving experience. The knowledge base grew over time as more problems were solved and more ATCs worked through NNABLE instead of independently or over the phone. NNABLE facilitated organizational memory by creating its own knowledge base for others to draw on.

The computer-supported intentional learning environment (CSILE) is an example of the creative combination of learning systems and performance support for use in schools. The Ontario Institute for Studies in Education developed CSILE to focus on collaborative learning (within groups or teams) and organizational memory (building an ever-increasing knowledge base within a school community).[5] CSILE encourages students to create their own store of learning, collected from both individual and group efforts. Individual students contribute to the knowledge base as authors and are acknowledged when others use their ideas. Collaboration is bred into the effort, as is the idea of a growing body of knowledge that current and future students can access in very flexible ways. CSILE is geared toward knowledge *creation* rather than knowledge *recitation*. Some classrooms already use the system, with impressive results. CSILE shows us what is possible when learning is closely linked with daily performance, allowing participants to capture what is learned and share the results across an organization.

The adventure of learning, with the technologies to support it, is inextricably woven into daily life at work and at home. Learning is now too important to be separated from the rest of existence.

21

Variations on the
Theme of Time

We usually think about time in terms of stages in life ("until the kids get out of college"), or regular increments ("every few years"), or other blocks that make sense and are realistic. The time-compressed business world also demands that we think about our work experiences in manageable chunks of time. Such mental devices are helpful, but they can lock us in to linear thinking along a strict continuum of beginning, middle, and end.

There are other ways of thinking about time and other ways of measuring it. Awakening in the morning, for example, brings with it a slow awareness of sensory impressions like the smell of coffee or the motion of dappled light against a shade. These impressions bring a sense of time, a complex interplay of memory and plan, sight, sound, and smell: the temporal present of the mind.

With the motion of getting up comes the knowledge that here is another day, this morning's light marking it off from last night's darkness. Today you will get up, brush your teeth, eat breakfast, go to work. Work is this day's progress on the project you will complete a week, a month, a year from now after that many more mornings like this one, that many more nights of sleep.

For corporate employees, getting up in the morning has been the beginning of daily routines basic to their individual lives. The week or the month is punctuated by pay—the salary, the dividend, unemployment insurance, the welfare or benefit check. Such payments represent yet other cycles, of labor done, of dates passed, of seasons on seasons for generations gone. They symbolize security. Many laid-off middle managers report that they still follow their old routines, getting up at the same time, dressing for the office, leaving the house and returning at the same times, even when such regularity is unnecessary and there is no office to go to.

Each punctuated tick of a clock marks off, in the way of human timekeeping, the nonretraceable passage toward death, delineating the very substance of time. Without the ticking there is no time as we have come to know it, and an awareness and understanding of time is vital both to our sense of self and the meaning of our labor. We therefore make plans for the day, the week, the year, the rest of our lives. The hands of the analog clock move regularly around to the right, what we call clockwise, just as we read (in English) from left to right. Remember, though, that what we call "clockwise" is arbitrary, not natural or predetermined by physics. "Clockwise" is an accident, as Brian Arthur has pointed out.[1] In 1443 the Renaissance painter Paolo Uccello designed a twenty-four-hour clock that ran counterclockwise. Only the weight of custom, the cumulative effect of using a certain configuration over time, has established the twelve-hour clock that runs to the right. In the same way, timekeeping is cultural in its origins, a concatenation of accidental events. Only slowly in the course of human history did time become the steady and predictable phenomenon we grew up believing it was, a belief reinforced by the digital clock, which marks time with the regularity of electromagnetic physics.

Time can be measured only by comparing two events that happen concurrently—the movement of the hands of a clock and the arrival of a friend, nightfall and dinner. Clock hands have no meaning by themselves, but in relation to human activity they have set a reassuring pulse for hundreds of years.

Human beings may take credit for inventing the cultural awareness of time, but it would be more accurate to suggest that a sense of time is wired into their genetic and neurophysiological makeup. There are many kinds of time. You may spontaneously take from the refrigerator what you will make for breakfast this morning (marking biological time). You may dream of building a house, and recorded in that threadlike chain of thought and feeling that makes up the continuity of life, you may hire an architect, help prepare the plans, watch the house come into being, move in, maintain, grow more complete and comfortable with the environment you have created, put up photographs of your parents that you will someday contemplate from your deathbed (mental time). You may prepare a will leaving your property to your children, even arrange to skip a generation and benefit *their* children, according to your conception of social time, your vision of the society that will continue after your death. Native American traditions stretched their idea of time over the next seven generations in making plans for the future.

We think we know that time is an arrow, don't we? Time, we have seen, goes die-straight from a known beginning to a predictable end.

It is an interesting coincidence that the word *die* can be the verb meaning to expire, to cease living, and the noun signifying a device used to cut or stamp out material, a template (which comes from the Greek *templo*, meaning a period, season, or time). A die and a template are both markers used for forming objects that will ultimately disintegrate. Time and the ticking of the clock are the same. And as far as we know, death is the last tick for us—when the clock stops, it is too poignantly true that the die is then cast. The linear idea of narrative time gave rise to the Western concept of unlimited progress that continues to mold and color our actions today.

But time is not an arrow at all. It is the cycle of day and night, summer and winter, life and death—all the dichotomies that make up the rise and fall of individuals and of civilizations, the birth and death of stars, perhaps even the grand cycle of the universe itself, from big bang to heat death to big bang again (depending on how much dark matter there is). It is the cycle of generations arising, and after propagating new generations, disappearing; the cycle of planting and harvesting, of boom and bust. In the cycle of geological time, what John McPhee in *Basin and Range* calls "deep time," mountains are thrust up from the earth and worn away again by rain and wind. In Ecclesiastes, the wind itself blows first to the south, then around to the north, and again, over and over, without end.

Business cycles we know about. Recession leads to recovery, we believe. And, of course, after recovery comes another recession.

We have suggested in Part II that it is helpful to consider other ways of thinking about time. If we think about the stages in our children's lives, for instance, these epochs can affect the way we work, the amount of time we work, where we work. When our children are young (or our parents are old), we may decide we must spend more time with them. Martha Wagner, whom we discussed in Chapter 17, listened to her children tell her how to divide her time. Check the voice mail after we're in bed, they told her. If you rearrange your time, you rearrange your priorities.

We have many ways of thinking about time, ways embedded in our proverbs. Time is money, so we can spend it—or waste it. Time devours all things. Time is the father of truth. Time has wings; it is here, then it is gone. Time and tide wait for no man. Lose an hour in the morning and you'll be all day hunting for it. Time is a thief, too.

Work is meaningful time because it translates into coin, at so much an hour. We ask, "May I have a few moments of your time?" Those moments won't have value unless we know what they are, how all the varieties of time clash and intersect.

The novelist Ann Lamott tells a story about going shopping with a friend who was in the late stages of terminal cancer. Watched by her friend, Ann tried on a dress. She looked at herself in the store mirror, then asked, "Does it make my hips look too big?"

Her friend looked at her from her wheelchair and answered, "Annie, you don't have that kind of time."

Stories like this may bring us up short, help us rearrange our priorities, create a new balance, and a new tension, between love and work. After reorganization, and especially after layoffs, assumptions about time—how it is measured, what it's worth, how far ahead one should plan—are reconsidered.

For most people, time is embedded in language, and the sense of time is a function of this fact. Verb tense, for example, is not universal. Chinese and Japanese have no tense that corresponds to what is in English the future. Such languages use the present tense, adding a future marker, such as the word for "tomorrow." Perhaps the long-term strategic business thinking of the Japanese results from this cultural extension of present time, with projections for the future conceived of as happening in a broadly pictured Now. English too has this sense in constructions like "Tomorrow I am going to New York." Awareness of how language shapes such conceptions is helpful, especially for members of cross-cultural teams.

What about long-term versus short-term priorities? The culture of short-term perspectives still prevails. In tight economic times, there are stronger-than-ordinary pressures to define success in terms of quarterly returns. A short-term crunch cannot go on indefinitely, but how long will it take before organizations realize that business is a long-term game?

Wall Street had better listen; it too doesn't have that kind of time. We know about Rome's building; we know about planting and harvesting, each in its time. We had better know about the cycles of human labor, also, because our time frame is shrinking toward zero.

Bill Walsh uses the phrase "urgent patience" to characterize his management style. It also describes the feeling he created within his organization.[2] There is an inherent dilemma here typical of the nineties: time-driven urgency is a fact of life, but the ability to reflect on options and implications and *not* jump into decisions until it is really necessary is critical for successful managers.

We need to build beliefs and attitudes about what is urgent and what is important into our corporate cultures. One of the keys to Walsh's success in coaching the San Francisco Forty-Niners football team was his ability to motivate for immediate action, yet continue to reflect on options and think through alternatives. The phrase "urgent patience" intentionally juxtaposes opposites to describe what Walsh sees as a mandatory balancing of short- and long-term views. Success in business requires the same balance of urgency and patience. In business today, urgent styles are everywhere, but patience is rare.

Patience is difficult in a time-pressed culture like ours. Biological processes have their own rhythms that are tied to the cycles of day and night, of the moon and the tides and the solar year. But the computers we work with operate on clocks that run to the thousands of cycles per second. That speed increases with each new generation of computer processors. Through the information technologies they have spawned, computers step up the pace of the ticking. As we grow into a symbiotic relationship with such speed, pressure builds on our biotemporality. Our attention is directed at shortening time: product cycles, production cycles, learning cycles, all are speeding up in what Jeremy Rifkin has called the "nanosecond culture."[3] We expect things to be, in the words of an old advertisement, "quicker than instant." Most of today's information technologies are pressure amplifiers, not relievers.

They need not be so. They may assist us instead, helping us to alter our perspectives on time and the business processes governed by it. If we don't learn this lesson, our technologies may force the change on us. We cannot possibly keep up, and we should not try. We need to learn where the threshold of urgency is. We need to learn patience, take time out to get a longer view, fit our immediate concerns into a broader time picture. As in traditional native American culture, we need to take a seven-generation view. That way we may avoid the consequences of too-hasty action: global warming, unforeseen pollution, imbalances of supply and demand.

A longer view can give us a clearer picture. Technology can speed us up to the point that we miss it, or it can help us see. For example, the U.S. Department of Transportation has developed a system for tracking and modeling air traffic flow across the United States. Each aircraft carries a small transponder that sends data back to the Volpe Transportation Research Center in Cambridge, Massachusetts. A screen the size of that in a large movie theater displays traffic flow in a room called "the Pit." Observers can zoom in or out to understand overall patterns.

This form of macro-modeling gives a longer view than is possible working from the bottom up (as individual air traffic controllers do). It increases the complexity of time relationships, and the urgency of action to prevent collisions, but at the same time it opens up the very concept of time, allowing us to make adjustments based on greater advance notice of possible conflicts.

It is important in this context to remind ourselves that people in other ages have devoted much of their finite time to the contemplation of eternity, and that there are other rhythms, even states wholly outside time, apparent to the human mind. These longer cycles may offer an antidote to the dis-ease created by the nanosecond culture. The time it takes a central processor to calculate ballistics tables is different, in quantity and kind, from the time of a human lifespan.

In 1990 the Honda Motor Company decided to give back to diverse American communities some of what it has earned in the U.S. market. Through the American Honda Education Corporation it has established Eagle Rock School, a high school residency program in Colorado for up to 96 students recruited mainly from impoverished school districts on Indian reservations, in inner cities, and in rural areas.

Robert Burkhardt, the head of the school, says Honda is committed to supporting Eagle Rock indefinitely. "The Japanese think in decades or centuries," he comments. "They aren't going to walk away from all this. This place will outlast my lifetime." The campus in Estes Park is nearing completion, and the first students are already in residence. The school has no endowment, but Burkhardt isn't concerned. "If something needs to be done, the money will be there. If it doesn't need to be done, then why budget the money?"

There is no immediate profit for Honda in Eagle Rock. Money, substantial amounts of it, flow into it. In the long term there will be graduates, of course, who will owe a dramatic change in their lives to a "foreign" corporation. They may be grateful. Honda may get some small short-term positive publicity from its largesse, but that alone would hardly account for such long-term plans. A few hundred potential customers for Honda would not justify the Wall Street approach, focusing as ever on the bottom line of the current financial statement.

Such a long-term sense of social time is unusual in business. What Honda knows is that without the ability to reframe our understanding of time from the short run to the long, from the linear to the cyclic, our institutions will have lifespans as evanescent as the mayfly's. There is, in this longer view, something called "quality," as in "quality of life." Wall Street time this is not.

22

Growing

Continuity

With the downsized, virtual corpo-
ration losing continuity as middle managers leave, new organizational
memory cells are evolving from an attention to learning, even if it
means relearning. Memory itself is not important. What is important is
recall, remembering what is needed when it is needed. Also, memory
itself is static; what organizations really need is animated memory that
supports the business processes.

Through restructuring and reengineering, business memory cells
are dispersing. Smaller and smaller proportions of organizational
memory are contained in filing cabinets, storage boxes, or the brain
cells of long-term employees. Memory has gone virtual, scattered
throughout the global fishnet of electronic and human communication.

We know that most organizations have poor memories, implicitly
inviting newer workers to make the same old mistakes. For organizations to learn, they must remember and communicate lessons to others. Efforts like Apple's Electronic Campus and CSILE suggest what is
possible rather than reflect mainstream practices. They raise this important question: What does an organization want to remember and
what does it want to forget?

Remembering too much may freeze an organization's creativity.
After all, innovation can grow out of having a bad memory. If people
don't know things are done in a certain way, they may discover a
better way. The term *organizational memory* has both positive and negative connotations.

We must also understand how to differentiate between what should
be remembered and what should be forgotten. Just as methods of

cultivating a garden change over time, practices develop from season to season. It is best to forget some practices when better ones are discovered.

Jim Parker, the repotted finance nomad, works in several virtual companies. One, a biotechnology start-up, owns nothing. All its scientific equipment is leased from a venture company that specializes in providing such equipment. The company's building is leased, and its phones. Payroll is outsourced. Jim comes in as a contractor, filling in until the company either is viable (in which case he will help find his replacement and move on) or closes its doors.

This company is little more than an idea for a product in its founders' minds. Venture capital is helping these backers turn that idea into reality. But what holds all this virtuality together so that something actually gets done?

To extend the horticultural metaphor, the new business organization must adopt practices analogous to those of French intensive gardening. New memory cells must grow in an environment that fosters a sense of organizational continuity, despite geographical and temporal dispersion. Since memory cannot exist without an awareness of time, this must be one of the chief nutrients for the new memory cells. Continuity is animated organizational memory.

Continuity is a product of the ability, culture, composite needs, desires, attitudes, and experiences of the people who make up an organization. In the interlinked complexity of the emerging global business culture, we all need a sense of balance and of being centered. For individuals, continuity requires a balance among work, home, leisure, and community, and between oneself and one's view of reality. By introducing new options, the anytime/anyplace office creates a sense of imbalance. But at the same time, the capabilities of information systems offer new potential for building continuity. (See Figure 22-1.)

In the midst of this turmoil, where urgent need meets emerging capability, a new form of organizational balance is emerging. This balance demands more than technological or mechanical metaphors. New metaphors must move beyond individual or team support to consider support for organizations and, ultimately, communities. How might information systems provide a nucleus for organizational and personal continuity? How might information systems support building, growing, and maintaining relationships?

Continuity is how things work in real time when they are in sync. It is a succession of events making a coherent whole, a balanced flow of energy, people, work processes, and production that benefits all the participants in a system.

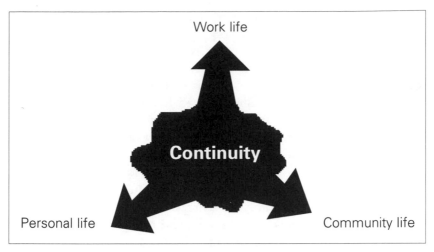

Figure 22-1 The dominant issue in the fishnet organization is continuity

Meanwhile, the quest for continuity will also involve a balancing of work and personal priorities. Ultimately, personal continuity will be valued most. How do work and home activities fit in with what each individual defines as important?

Ann Wentworth is a member of a team managing real estate holdings for an alliance of investment portfolios, an Israeli trading company with headquarters in Singapore, and a small high-tech firm in Texas, which is designing a shared filing system for such coalitions.

Ann lives in Billings, Montana. Her business takes her all over the world, although she seldom travels. She finds it exciting to work with people around the globe, even though she has seen most of them only through her desktop video system.

At the moment, however, she's annoyed. The message on her screen reads, "Property taxes are due on parcel 76654 in Arcata, Illinois," highlighted in a virulent electronic lavender that makes it seem all the more peremptory. A window on the monitor has opened to show the property in question, a strip mall whose major client is a virtual reality entertainment center.

Ann is busy bottle-feeding one of the calves on her ranch and at first ignores the message, but a mellow male voice keeps reciting it over and over, as if the system is afraid she'll miss the point.

"I'm coming," she shouts over her shoulder.

When she finishes with the calf she puts down the bottle and goes to the console, frowning at the text. This is one of those times she almost regretted installing the workstation in the barn. Finally she touches the screen to stop the voice.

"I know, I know," she says aloud. "And I've already done it!"

She types a message to VISOR (the cutesy name her team has given its work-flow support system): "Check written and sent, last Friday." (It's perhaps ironic that she should need to write out a check when electronic payment is so much faster and more efficient, but some states—she can never remember exactly which ones—still insist on a paper trail, so some checks are still written by hand.)

A shared database of the group members' various "to dos" relating to real estate management, VISOR tracks all such transactions and automatically sends bimonthly status reports to the appropriate team members. Paying taxes is at the routine end of the spectrum, though with so many properties, missing tax deadlines and paying penalties were frequent before the VISOR system was introduced, and the amounts were significant.

Now Ann must send a bug report to the company in Texas. "Record," she says.

"Recording," the computer answers. She looks into the camera and makes her statement. "And tell it to quit talking at me. I know what I'm doing," she finishes. "Send that off."

"Where?" the computer says. This time the question makes sense, and she answers.

There are many other reasons VISOR has paid off. The members of Ann's team can stay in close communication with each other, but even more important, teams across the alliance use the same processes for managing holdings and comparing results. VISOR also analyzes patterns to identify trends and provides background for reviews of team performance.

The calf starts bawling again, and Ann swears at VISOR under her breath. "Sometimes the damn thing is a real pain in the neck," she bluntly concedes, but without it the meta-teams making up her company would be unable to work in concert. The alternative is chaos—or even worse, frequent flyer clubs.

Even in the mid-nineties, Ann's situation is not unusual. She works for a company that is not a company in any traditional sense. Yet it is work she likes, and she is getting paid well for it.

But continuity is a problem for Ann and her sort-of-a-company. How can a company that doesn't have a physical center establish any kind of continuity? The systems that are becoming the core technologies of day-to-day work must balance flexibility with reasonable constraints as work processes change. The danger is that they will be seen as fixed structures.

A chair is balanced, but it is hard to move when you are sitting in it. Organizational continuity is more like a bicycle than a chair, a system with dynamic balance that is controlled by a user. Unfortunately, today's continuity systems are more like chairs, or maybe tricycles, balanced and stable but slow and inflexible. Continuity is essential to keep bureaucracies from solidifying and allowing organizations to innovate and grow, but designers and users should avoid the trap of thinking that technology will relieve human beings of the continual job of learning and understanding each other and their customers. Aids to continuity (work-flow tracking systems, reengineering methods), like bicycles, are simply tools. The artistry is up to us.

Nonetheless, technologies that help coordinate work flow can relieve a wide range of organizational and end-user stress in tasks like managing budget cycles, reporting, and so on. Most organizations have bottlenecks in their work processes that impede effective operations. These processes need lubrication: they squeak painfully now, and without help will seize up permanently in the near future. In the coming age of team-based organizations, particularly those with many outside alliance partners and geographically dispersed operations, it will be vital to glue together those parts of the organization that are charged with key functions. Organizational continuity is not just a desire; it is a demand.

Continuity implies not only appreciation for the past but anticipation of the future. Such an overview of time asks us to suspend temporarily our awareness of the present in order to look at a continuous flow from past to future.

The data on which decisions were based in the traditional organization were only snapshots in time. Flexibility and nimbleness are required in the global work environment to negotiate a moving picture of change and crisis. Even the executives who remain to run the new organizations will not be hermetically isolated decision makers; they will be at the center of collaborative processes. The lubrication for these processes will come increasingly from former middle managers who are able to view problems through their acquired sense of history, continuity, and a coherent whole.

Having to track several projects at the same time and needing new tools to do it, surviving middle managers will also make innovations in methods of maintaining continuity. Users, vendors, and consultants will customize work-flow software packages to support new patterns.

Organizations in the information era must be structured enough to allow people and groups to work together but still encourage free-spirited inquiry. They must deal creatively with uncertainty instead of futilely trying to eliminate it. Effective organizations will strike a balance that allows them not only to accept uncertainty but to take advantage of it. Ann Wentworth did not particularly like the way VISOR guided the flow of her work, but she accepted it as a fact of life. Doing without it was unthinkable. Ideally, continuity systems will be positive aids that enhance organizations' flexibility without overly constraining individuals.

Organizations need some degree of structure to perform well. Even far-out R&D organizations that are advancing technological frontiers have accepted procedures for group work and production and for balancing open inquiry with cooperative work. Bill Griebstein, a former manager of research and development at Procter and Gamble, refers to the balancing point as the "ragged edge of chaos." Continuity need not be comfortable. Context can be complex.

Continuity, the flow from past to future, forces attention on the various concepts and aspects of time. Information encompasses time, timeliness, and quality. Moving at the speed of light around the globe, it promotes both greater timeliness and higher quality. The time-aware manager will feel the pulse of the syncopated rhythms of the world, from the nanosecond culture of the computer to generational thinking of social time to the centuries of historical time in the continuous process of evolution itself.

The longer view asks us to develop incentives beyond those that develop naturally. For example, some senior managers of flexible organizations could establish explicit reward structures that extend beyond normal business cycles. A sales organization might be managed by a person whose rewards are based on three-year returns and ongoing client relationships.

As mentioned in the previous chapter, native Americans used to think of future time as extending through the next seven generations. We too would benefit from thinking generations ahead. Such a detached perspective puts the time-compressed, time-harassed worker at ease. An organization could achieve continuity over succeeding generations by allowing workers to alter and stretch their orientation toward quality and time.

Meanwhile business organizations of the information era increasingly nurture and reward the skills of generalists rather than deep knowledge in a specific field. Those who can adapt quickly to new situations, the "quick studies" who deliver consistently, will be successful. Speed is not velocity but a quality of attention, of focus, that is narrowed in its time dimension and deepened in its intensity. Those who want to develop expertise in specialized areas will find it more difficult to apply their knowledge within the swirling array of intra- and inter-corporate teams. Companies may, if they do not take precautions, suffer a loss of expertise that could lower the quality of the end product.

Outside contractors will supply the necessary expertise in the emerging global organization. Free-lancers will be able to move swiftly and comfortably in the unstable flux of fishnet organizations where everything, as we know, is just in time. We float on the surface of many kinds of time, mostly unaware of the depths beneath us, but the more we know about the depths, the more confidence we will have in the quality of our work.

The future lies in how we come to understand the intricate relationship between time and quality: all the kinds of time, all the shapes of quality. Attention, focus, and above all, relationship will determine the outcome of today's efforts at defining the quality of tomorrow. The move in entire enterprises to examine how to achieve total quality communicates an underlying sense of stability ("We're in it for the long run"), which in turn provides a foundation for innovation and new incentives for individual and team performance.

Many fishnet organizations extend far beyond any given company or industry. Building continuity is not easy, but it is necessary to provide context for more specific actions. Continuity is, in effect, the environment in which virtual organizations have their existence. Sune Karlsson, vice president of Asea Brown Boveri, says of his organization, "We are not a global business. We are a collection of local businesses with intense global continuity."[1]

23

Growing
Community

Communities are changing faster than their citizens can keep up. The very idea of "us" and "them" has blurred beyond recognition. Even the broader categories in which we have traditionally grouped people are breaking down. People are demanding recognition for who they are, who their ancestors were, their geographical origins. The category "Asian Americans" does not distinguish Vietnamese Americans, or Indian Americans, or Hmong, Lao, Thai, Cambodian, Chinese, or Japanese Americans. Latin Americans are not, as Dan Quayle once implied, people who speak Latin; they speak in the dialects of Argentina, Peru, Cuba, Mexico, and Puerto Rico.

U.N. Ambassador Madeleine Albright refers to NATO as "the best alliance in the world," one that many nations are now clamoring to join. She insists that the basis of NATO's effectiveness is not its size, its military capability, or its financial resources, but the mutual respect and understanding of its member countries. Belgium is small, Germany large, but each country plays an equal role in the alliance. This value accorded to individual distinctiveness is especially suited to the post–cold war world. It is the primary value of the emerging global community.

An electronically enhanced community is arising in Japan. Morihiko Hiromatsu, the governor of Oita, has electronically connected all the homes in his prefecture in pursuit of a vision he calls "gross national satisfaction." The regional economy has been reorganized so as to distribute tasks and responsibilities equitably. Each village, with its own specialty, fits into an interdependent fishnet structure connecting individuals in the various communities. Not high-tech wizardry but only basic telephone, text, and commercial transaction capabilities have enabled Oita to implement this vision of community.

Whereas individuals in the United States struggle to learn how to work in teams and U.S. organizations scramble to find ways to reward them, teams have been part of Japanese culture for centuries. The design of continuity systems in Japan can thus proceed from the top down, and in the process contribute to community.

In the United States we are grappling with the notion of electronic democracy, electronic town halls, and the many ways in which communities might use the new media to enhance participation in public affairs. Within the next decade we will reach a watershed when voters will be able to cast their ballots electronically on virtually any issue. At this point an awkward fact will become manifest. Until now politicians have claimed that direct democracy is in principle a wonderful idea but cannot work in practice because it is impossible for everyone's voice to be registered on all issues, and so our governmental system is a representative one. Soon, when everyone *could* vote on any issue that arises in the electronic forum, we will have to decide what kind of democracy we really want. Shall we take a poll?

The word *community* is now hot in Silicon Valley, where researchers see more than a vision of an electronically linked web of people who work, live, and play together in an ethereal space in which the whole is greater than the sum of the parts. As anytime/anyplace work becomes more common, the divisions between work and leisure grow ever more tangled.

Moreover, our communities are becoming more diverse. Many companies already have culturally diverse workforces with high percentages of black, Hispanic, Asian, and female workers. With the emergence of a global community, however, thorny problems appear. One hopes that information technologies can help bridge diversity and provide learning opportunities for people who have been left out of the mainstream. There is some basis for this hope, since information technologies are becoming powerful aids to learning and communication. But there are no easy solutions; diversity is a dilemma, with both attractive and ugly aspects.

Those striking out into the new world where neither culture nor colleagues are stable will find themselves not only trying to keep their own learning up and running but also coaching and assisting an increasingly diverse network of fellow workers, offering informal ad hoc training as the need arises. Managing diversity will be a full-time job for anyone with a niche in the interlinked economy.

If managing diversity comes to be viewed as a business issue rather than an ethical one, minorities might actually fare better. Because the biggest labor shortage crises are still a few years off, it will take a long-term view to prompt corporations to act now. The trend toward establishing quick-fix business teams will work against taking a longer view. It is increasingly up to the individual to pick up the slack and act swiftly, doing well by doing good.

Companies with a serious interest in the goals of affirmative action or exploiting the diverse labor force of the nineties must change both strategy and tactics. Strategically, a commitment to hiring minorities may require special efforts to train people who lack the necessary skills. The need to provide such training may lower a company's ability to compete in the marketplace in the short run and test the degree of its commitment to affirmative action, but in the long run companies that make this investment will have an advantage as the proportion of minorities in the workforce increases.

In the short run, diversity challenges formal programs, such as the affirmative action programs of the past, that are intended to bring groups together. In the electronic community, these efforts will either fall short or miss the mark entirely. But diversity can strengthen the interlinked organizations of the future. In a diverse marketplace, a diverse workforce can be a distinct asset.

Successful organizations will be sensitive to the unique needs and interests of workers of differing cultural backgrounds. This is a unique and irreplaceable opportunity. Not only can minorities help an organization find its way into new markets as the formerly disenfranchised move into the interlinked economy, but their very worldview, their attitudes and assumptions, is an information resource.

Fishnet organizations make it easier for outsiders to move into important positions. Flexible, interlinked organizations reorganize frequently, and opportunities to enter the fast track are likely to come more often than in yesterday's hierarchical organizations. Women, minorities, older workers—all kinds of people of diverse backgrounds will have the chance to move ahead. At the same time, formal affirmative action programs are likely to be weakened considerably in the move toward flexible organizations. Immediate business goals will supersede long-term goals for affirmative action. If a member of a business team cannot produce results quickly, where is the incentive to train her rather than turn to a temporary employee who is ready and available? We must not only cope with diversity; we must make it work for us.

Government will play only a small role. Even an administration in Washington that strongly supports affirmative action will have trouble keeping tabs on flexible organizations, so responsibility for achieving greater inclusiveness is likely to move from the government or corporate level to the tactical level of specific decisions that individual managers make as they form teams. It is difficult to imagine a scenario in which most companies will enthusiastically promote affirmative action as a matter of policy. It is equally difficult to imagine government enforcement of affirmative action requirements in the amorphous fishnet organization. A few high-principled companies will strike out on their own to meet these targets, but labor force opportunism will be much more common.

Corporations that realize that diversity is a permanent fact of life will begin to recast the problem as an opportunity. Organizations that pass up the chance to bring these vast groups into the workforce and the marketplace will ultimately lose out to companies that are more willing to train and educate those who will make up both the consumer and the labor forces of the future. Without the full-hearted participation of everyone in the interlinked economy, we will all be the poorer.

It may be that the fact of diversity will help organizations pioneer new, nonmonetary methods of compensating work and encouraging loyalty and stability. In the long run, such methods may well be both cheaper for employers and more satisfying for employees. Increased employee loyalty will be particularly valuable to far-flung global corporations, where it is vital that team members have clear incentives to cooperate.

Varied career paths will allow for diverse needs and work patterns. For example, by the year 2000 there will be almost eighteen million workers over age fifty-five. Creative part-time or contractual arrangements could make good use of this base of experience.

Working across ethnic and national borders complicates cultural mismatches. One of our colleagues at the Institute for the Future, Mary O'Hara-Devereaux, is a psychologist who has worked in twenty-five different countries during her career. That staggering experience has led her to conclude that what she calls "absence of context" is one of the key barriers to successful cross-cultural work. Lack of a common cultural groundwork is highlighted in the story about the international architectural team in Chapter 13. The Italian Luigi Cirasola comes from a high-context culture, meaning that many of the important things about a situation go unstated and there is a high value placed on human relationships and harmony. By contrast, Perry Wilcox's mainstream American culture, overlaid by elements of the Texas subculture, is low-context; people expect things to be explicit, punctual, and results oriented. In trying to work together, both Luigi and Perry suffer from an absence of context. Neither understands where the other is coming from. What is most direct for one culture is not for the other. As O'Hara-Devereaux points out, "The quickest route from A to B may not be a straight line if there is a cultural cliff in between."[1]

Culture embodies the critical underlying values and norms that guide both the daily behavior of individuals and the business strategies of corporations. Culture shapes thinking, feeling, and acting. It provides context, the frame of reference that gives meaning to a situation. Perry realized later that the absence of a common context had caused the misunderstanding with Luigi over when the revised factory plans would be finished. He had lost his temper over something the person on the other end of the international phone connection had not even noticed.

Frames of reference shape what we perceive and how comfortable we are in working and communicating with others. They are related to personal values and cultural backgrounds, but they have more to do with the *process* of perceiving and making judgments, which varies from one individual to another. Some frames are rigid, with many assumptions built in; others are flexible. The role of leaders of organizations is to establish a shared frame of reference—or at least an acceptance of different frames of reference, and a means of bridging them.

For international workers or those whose jobs bring them into frequent contact with people of different cultural backgrounds, being able to see one's habits through someone else's eyes is crucial. Every individual has a frame of reference, a point of view from which he sees the world. Members of work teams must develop a way of understanding and communicating across the different frames of reference that exist within any new organization.

When the middle manager leaves the fold, voluntarily or not, she takes an essential resource: her Rolodex. A new definition of corporate loyalty is loyalty to one's Rolodex, the individuals it lists, the floats that keep the personal fishnet oriented and available. The personal Rolodex may overlap with the corporate one; in fact, it probably will. This means that the personal and corporate fishnets will overlap as well. We can see this in the numbers of former middle managers who find themselves consulting for either companies they have left or their former companies' competitors. Whether it is a physical or an electronic file, the Rolodex lists the nodes of workers' community fishnets.

In the new business environment, workers' loyalty is to the web of people with whom they have collaborated successfully. And those with consulting contracts may find that they have more job security than full-time—formerly called "permanent"—employees. Each social network registered in a Rolodex forms the context for future work projects. New forms of community are growing, and old ones are being recast in new settings. Future communities will be made up of both familiar and new faces connected through a variety of media in an ever-changing pattern.

24

Toward Electronic

Commerce

Electronic Commerce" is a tag that has been used heavily by the start-up company General Magic in introducing a new environment called Telescript. We hope that the term doesn't become identified with any single product, however, since its wider application is important to both emerging organizational forms and consumers.

Electronic commerce means exchanging products, ideas, and services over electronic networks, which provide an infrastructure that facilitates the exchange. The vision has been around for decades under a variety of names, but it is just now becoming practical on a large scale. Ted Nelson calls his Xanadu; another example was the ill-fated start-up venture AMIX—electronic transactions for everyone.

Bottom-line results drove the hierarchical corporations of traditional businesses. Measures of outcome were the primary indicators of success. As recent moves toward total quality have shown, however, focusing on the work process is often more productive than being obsessed with outcomes. If the process is right, good outcomes follow. This shift in perspective is difficult for many managers to make, especially those who started out and became successful in companies organized in the hierarchical model of the industrial age. Hierarchies are still home for many of us, for better or for worse. But as the physical objects of our commerce disappear and become virtual material for the information economy, commerce itself turns electronic.

Here is one situation we encountered: John Murata, a single-proprietor member of an international construction team, is working late.

It is nearly midnight on the West Coast, and he has only two more hours to get in his bid for a 5:00 P.M. deadline in Bangkok.

Although he currently participates with varying degrees of intensity on three other teams, John leads this team and regards it possessively. Its work has been terrific. Two days earlier the team members learned from their intelligence database that a competitor, the Agora Group, had been talking with the government of Thailand about a major new project. Since Agora knew it would have competition, it had persuaded the Thai government to set a very close deadline for project proposals. Although Agora's leaders claimed the rush was necessary because of the monsoon season, John knew that what they really wanted was to shut his team out. It was plain good luck that John's Russian alliance partner, APCo, was closer to the Asian scene than he was. Renata Davidoff, his partner at APCo, noticed the project and its deadline on the Internet before it was too late.

This is the first time John and APCo have worked together on a joint bid. He and Renata have pulled together previous development blueprints and tenders and come up with a great proposal. The team's draft of the tender and pricing documents have just arrived. Now John has two hours to finalize them. There are a few potential problems he still needs to check against his current knowledge bases.

He types furiously, calling up on the computer screen the proper wording for the joint bid. This is important since he and APCo represent two different kinds of legal entities governed by the laws of two different countries. The knowledge base includes joint bids made with other alliance partners, some of which turn out to be applicable to this bid.

He checks the pricing and payment arrangements of the proposal against future financial planning models and currency predictions, presented in the form of computer-generated visualizations. Not only can he work out the answers to his questions quickly, but also he can share the results visually, which works much better across cultures. The information allows him to improve the pricing structure and make the bid more competitive.

Finally he checks the current and predicted tax policies for the three countries involved. Again, tax policy calls for a significant change in the documents. A mistake in calculating projected taxes would be costly—paying unanticipated taxes could easily eat up all the profits from the project.

When John signs and faxes the documents, he's feeling confident about the bid. It arrives in Thailand before the deadline and wins the job.

Electronic media are seeping into the cracks in the traditional business infrastructure. Computers and telecommunications are creating new borders. Domains on the Internet, for example, have cryptic labels like "org" (for nonprofit organizations), "com" (communications groups), "gov" (government, of course), and "edu" (educational institutions.) The borders between these domains are fluid, almost transparent; they are, in fact, little more than signposts to identity.

This means we are still on a frontier. Electronic networks may be more subversive of traditional divisions than all the intentional restructuring and reengineering in the world.

Though there has been strong opposition to commercial uses of the Internet, more and more individuals are earning a living by harvesting and repackaging information from it. An electronic marketplace is being born, a frontier of electronic commerce. The Internet has more than ten million "inhabitants" already, and its population is growing rapidly. These users, of course, are not representative of the population at large. They are, however, early pioneers exploring the limits and possibilities of network communities. Some of the most important probes of the future are happening right now, even though most businesspeople have only a vague understanding of what the Internet is all about. (See Figure 24-1.)

In fact, nobody fully understands the Internet. It is so large and growing so organically that understanding it is impossible, let alone controlling it. As we remarked in Chapter 2, the Internet is more like a termite mound than a highway. It is a throbbing, breathing, growing community life form and a fascinating environment for learning about future options today.

Taking a pragmatic step back from the public Internet, McKesson Corporation is using computers for coordinating traditional business transactions and reducing their cost. While McKesson's network is far less complex than the Internet, its commercial sophistication is greater.

It is thus useful to assess early business ventures into the world of electronic commerce. Eric Clemons of the Wharton School of Business has concluded that the effects of such ventures are profound: "The improved ability to monitor performance of outside vendors, combined with reduced risk associated with reliance upon outsiders, is resulting in increased use of outsourcing and of cooperative ventures more generally. We see this as effectively changing the boundary of firms, and ultimately altering the structure of some industries."[1]

When firms go global, corporate boundaries change at least as much as national ones. The nature of these changes is unpredictable and be-

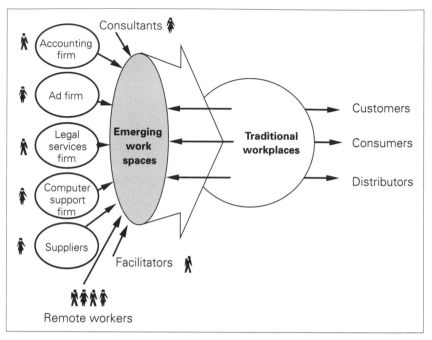

Figure 24-1 Electronic commerce will develop in an organizational context that looks like this

yond individual or corporate control. New frontiers are opening, creating new threats and new opportunities. Electronic commerce makes all borders transparent and wildly flexible.

Business teams can benefit from dynamic corporate boundaries, but the same managers leading the drive for flexible business teams are likely to cringe and strike back violently when, for example, security violations occur. This is a crisis waiting to happen as companies are forced to think about where to try to draw lines. Individual contractors must also be flexible to respond to these changing boundaries, shifting borders, and an increasingly prevalent frontier mentality.

The anytime/anyplace office is part of the picture. Electronic commerce introduces basic questions about how work itself is organized. For example, employees have traditionally traveled to their work, but there are alternatives. Mark Stefik and John Seely Brown of Xerox Palo Alto Research Center (PARC) advance the notion of "portable ideas," the moving of ideas instead of people.[2] After all, commodities exist only in electronic bits. It doesn't matter—literally—where the employee is.

Anytime/anyplace work makes more radical options possible. As we move toward twenty-four-hour global businesses and markets, the anytime/anyplace office may be the means by which companies take advantage of multiple time zones. Work will be transported not just to employees, but to employees in the right time zone. Other decisions about location could be made with such factors in mind as business sites range out into the electronic world.

General Magic, founded by Marc Porat and several of the pivotal figures from the early history of the Apple Macintosh, has developed an interface and language for conducting electronic commerce. Telescript will facilitate interaction between human beings far distant from one another. Eventually, according to Andy Hertzfeld, one of the company's principals, software agents will go into the network for us, look for bargains, and do our negotiating for us, making deals without our help. These agents will then report back to us for approval.

At the heart of electronic commerce is the problem of how to pay for value received over such networks. Some infrastructure or service must document exchanges between buyers and sellers. Users' trust that the electronic marketplace will function fairly and accurately is a key element in making such a system work. Already it is possible to subscribe to some magazines by sending a credit card number over the Internet, but few trust the network security enough to do it.

Perhaps the "buy button" has been the simplest electronic commerce proposal. Added to a television set, telephone, or terminal, the button would access a user's credit account or other source of money. Some means of authentication would have to be developed so that not just any button pusher could make a purchase in the name of the owner of the device. The idea may be too simplistic to be practical, but it exemplifies the convenience that both buyers and sellers would like to have available. Another scheme, proposed by General Magic, is that a prospective customer would be able to send out an electronic request routed according to linkages drawn by a web of intelligent agents to match buyers and sellers.

Electronic commerce would be nothing less than a new way of conducting business. It is now a question of what such a system will look like, and who will develop (and make money from) the process, and how quickly we can get there.

We are on the verge of a practical infrastructure for electronic commerce—or, problematically, more than one. Telescript is the boldest step toward electronic commerce so far. The combination of its design characteristics and the partners contributing to its creation (including

Apple, AT&T, Philips, Motorola, NTT, Sony, and Matsushita) give it a strong chance of success, though it is still only a chance as yet. The return will be immense: electronic commerce will free human workers for more fulfilling activities as they build communities that integrate family, work, and leisure into a vital fishnet web.

25

Upsized Managers
and Downsized
Organizations

$\mathbf{M}$yths permeate our lives: the myth of Yankee ingenuity, the myth of the benevolent (or malevolent) corporation, the myth of the White Knight. We must recognize the power of myth if we are to forge new ones that are appropriate to our time. The myth of the wounded land helps us connect our immediate circumstances with historical change. In discovering that, like other lands in other times, our land is wounded, people can find example and solace in such essential stories about life.

Myth offers a way of beginning to understand, or at least accept, uncertainty. The concept of myth may be unfamiliar to many people in business, but myths exist there, too. Tracy Kidder's book *The Soul of a New Machine* told a myth of the computer industry, describing the adventures of a team creating a new product. Many figures in the computer industry loom larger than life: Doug Engelbart, Steve Jobs, Mitch Kapor, John Sculley, Regis McKenna. Every other industry likewise has such heroes, with lore about their doings usually passed on by word of mouth. These still-living figures also have everyday lives, of course, though their mythic lives are larger and often more compelling.

But outworn business myths can also limit the imagination. Most of us have unexamined assumptions about our organizations and how they work, as well as how to work with them. In the fishnet organization, we need powerful new myths to guide us.

In casual use, the word *myth* has come to mean a widely accepted fallacy. The accurate meaning of the term, however, is an extended metaphor, a story that helps the members of a culture understand certain truths. As Mircea Eliade, the pioneering scholar of world religions at the University of Chicago, puts it, "Myths reveal the structure of reality, and the multiple modalities of being in the world."[1]

To borrow an analogy from Silicon Valley, myths are the human equivalent of operating systems in computers. Like operating systems, they run below the surface to frame what is possible and to make sense out of the reality that all human beings share. The Public Broadcasting commentator Bill Moyers has called mythology "an interior road map of experience, drawn by people who have traveled it."[2]

We must all come to grips with our wounded land, for it is in just this kind of time that heroes arise. Both those who are laid off and those who survive cuts in their organizations have the chance to become heroes, even if reluctant ones. A period when the world's corporations are downsizing is just the time to consider upsizing the individual.

The traditional business organization is changing faster than most people can absorb or understand. These changes are upsetting everyone's balance, creating new stresses, and knocking both the manager and her familiar world out of place.

Many of the myths and metaphors that shape our thinking about business today are drawn from sports. The San Francisco Forty-Niners, the Boston Celtics, the Los Angeles Lakers, and the Oakland Raiders all create mythic images, even in the minds of those who do not follow sports closely. Sports analogies help people describe what goes on, or needs to go on, in their organizations. Business teams have "chalk talks" to plan new tasks; they speak of the "fast break" stage, when everyone on a team is going at full tilt; and they refer to the "final minutes," the "home stretch" as a team approaches its deadline. Military analogies are also common within some business cultures. Business is war (a metaphor), but if we discuss strategy in terms of Waterloo or Marathon or Valley Forge, we draw on the mythology of those famous battles to shape attitudes and opinions.

Sports myths and military myths, however, are worn and limited. They tend to hold more meaning for men than for women, more meaning for Americans than people from many other cultures. We need to move beyond sports stories and war stories as we think about future organizations.

Whether Henry Ford or Lee Iacocca, American businesspeople are captivated by solo heroes. Yet great successes in business are usually the result of team effort, not the work of a single individual. Secretary of Labor Robert Reich has argued that we need to think not just of individuals but of business teams themselves as heroes.[3] Successful teams need to become our new models, their members the heroes of new myths emulated by the teams that follow.

In the timeless world of myth, the hero is often born in humble circumstances: the son of a tailor, a widow, the daughter of a farmer, a factory worker. Or the protagonist may be the awkward prince or disobedient princess everyone ignores, the one with no prospects, the lonely one who daydreams of greater things but never does them. Certainly he or she is no hero.

Forces at work in the world rumble dimly in the distance: a dragon, a plague, a civil war ravages the countryside—something awful, yet safely beyond the limited local horizon. The remote evil cannot affect life in this small place, whether palace or shop. But then the danger comes closer. It may be a call for help, a brush with death, a neighbor or a friend destroyed. The hero does nothing at first. After all, he's nobody. If pressed, he might ask, "Why me?"

The budding hero is reluctant to change, to leave home, to try being something he is sure he is not. The familiar world may be going painfully awry, but the local surroundings are at least familiar. Hiding, however, grows increasingly untenable. This time what happens propels the hero out into the world and onto the journey. The imperial troops attack the farm, as in *Star Wars*, and Luke Skywalker is left homeless. Or the manager who has safely held on to her job until the current round of cuts is now herself laid off, or it is just too painful to stay any longer. The distant and abstract evil becomes vividly personal. The fear is real. The future is frightening: insecure, impoverished, and worst of all, desperately unknown.

The dynamic shift to global, interlinked, flexible fishnet organizations has brought with it anxiety and malaise. This is the sickness that threatens the land today. But everyone has the potential to become a hero one way or another, voluntarily or involuntarily. This forging of new myths for our age is, very simply, a matter of survival.

The hero crosses the threshold of fear and steps into the unknown. The world will not work the way it always did before. Business won't offer the same kinds of opportunities, or give the same kinds of rewards. Those hoping to embark on a safe and predictable life path discover that the cottage has burned down and they are alone and friendless. The world of our parents is no more. We are on our own, cut off from the past in ways that we are only just beginning to understand.

The changes in the way we work over the past twenty years, and in the way we think about work, are not only difficult and unsettling; they are fundamental. Businesses are entering a time of great uncertainty, one in which massive organizational earthquakes are common: the fall of the bureaucracies of the Eastern bloc, the collapse of the savings and loan associations, for example.

This is not necessarily bad or unnatural. Earthquakes are frightening, but there are always survivors. One strategy for survival is to design structures that sway with the quaking earth instead of resisting it.

In the end, we are the creators of our public (and to a large extent, our private) selves, the inventors of the roles we choose to play. This means only that we may find, among the complex modalities of our personalities, a set of operating instructions for ourselves. We may find, in other words, an identity. If we no longer possess an ingrained quality called character, we must become one—a hero, perhaps.

Identity derives in part from the roles we play, so our first task is to determine what role suits us best, what personal strategy for long-term survival is most appropriate. In other words, before determining what the content of life is—what business or professional expertise we will acquire or practice—we must determine the shape that content will take. The chosen role is the answer to the question, What do you want to be when you grow, not to adulthood, but to the next stage in your life's journey? The answer is not "a fireman" or "a policeman"—those are professions—but "a warrior" or "a chief," "a wizard" or "a thief," for these are roles that exist within many different professions.

The sociologist Erving Goffman, whose book *The Presentation of Self in Everyday Life* was published in 1959, is a source of this perspective.[4] Goffman suggested that the overriding metaphor for the ways in which people interact is the theater, and that people play roles to impress or influence others. In other words, as we have already noticed in the world of electronic media, everything is *drama*. There are imposing roles—presidents and prime ministers, movie and rock stars, athletes, generals, swindlers, warlords and Mother Teresas, even an artist or two—and there are the smaller parts we all play as we angle for what Andy Warhol called each person's "fifteen minutes of fame."

We all are conscious of some of the roles we play: mother, son, friend, employee, teacher, student. Others may change in different contexts—home or office, public or private relationships.

The best-known type of hero is the Warrior. Clint Eastwood and Arnold Schwarzenegger play outward warriors in the movies. A true *inner* warrior, by contrast, may be a poet who simply knows how to stand her ground. She may be a poet by profession, but her role is that of the warrior. She is someone who, when she loses her job or sees the traditional structures of her culture—the familiar touchstones of content—crumble, manages to reevaluate the situation and go on. The news already tells about far too many laid-off Eastwood-style warriors who come back to the office with an Uzi to blow away former co-workers. Usually the most outwardly aggressive people are those who most sorely lack the qualities of the inner warrior. They let the outer world establish their worth, and meet any slight with hostility. The true warrior spirit is strong and fierce enough not to need the macho display or the outward reinforcement of ego. Its inner boundaries are secure.

As we first wrote this chapter, Michael Jordan announced his retirement from professional basketball. A supremely gifted athlete, a superstar and celebrity, a pitchman for shoes and shirts, Jordan provoked massive media attention when he made the announcement. The most common word used for Jordan by those in the vast call-in radio audience was "hero." His unmatched grace, skill, and expertise demonstrated the possibility of something better than what even the best players are often capable of. Most people, fans and nonfans alike, agreed that the world was a better place for having someone like him in it. Jordan then confirmed his true hero status by announcing that he was going to start over in a completely different sport, baseball, a new frontier for him, revealing that he is more interested in the hero's struggle than in the hero's reward. Whether or not he succeeded, Jordan took a classic hero's path. In his return to basketball in 1995, he began a new hero's journey.

Lesser heroes, individuals facing competition, failure, fear, and doubt, can aspire to the stature of Michael Jordan without needing or wanting the attendant fame. This is not the result of inspirational thinking or repeating some mantra in the tradition of Dale Carnegie. It is the way of the warrior in many traditions, of the person who does not give up, who pursues his goal until the end, win or lose.

The warrior is not necessarily a leader, though he is usually capable of independent action when needed. The warrior must be capable of cooperative effort, of teamwork. The warrior role often demands group effort. One kind of warrior is a person willing to submerge significant parts of herself for the good of the group—in other words, a follower, someone able to carry out whatever is asked of her. Not everyone is cut out to be a general. But whether they are leaders or followers, warriors are essential to the success of any social effort.

Another kind of role is that of the wizard: the person who gets things done and conceals the methods by which they are done. She is a kind of entrepreneur, middleman, or broker between two realities, with each foot in a different camp. This is a demanding role. Flexibility, problem solving, openness, and quickness are prized virtues. Like an anthropologist, the wizard lives in two very different realities and provides the bridge between them. In this sense the wizard may also be a kind of thief who can take what is needed in one realm from another in a way that benefits both. Though some of the wizard's work may depend on illusion, the smoke and mirrors of the Great Oz bellowing down at Dorothy and the others, the important part of the wizard's work is its results. When Dorothy accuses the Wizard of Oz of being a bad man, he replies that he is not a bad man, only a bad wizard. But in the end the Scarecrow, the Tin Man, the Lion, and Dorothy all get what they need, and the wizard turns out to be an effective entrepreneur after all, even though he is, in the end, only human. Or perhaps it is *because* he is human.

Hero roles are not necessarily from the fairy-tale land we associate with myth, the land of dragons and knights, castles and wizards. The explorer, the ever-curious person with a high tolerance for uncertainty, is a role firmly rooted in more recent times. The explorer is willing to take risks, to leave behind the familiar and comfortable, to investigate unusual or unlikely professional pursuits or relocate in an unusual place which may entail learning a new language or culture. The explorer is not afraid of solitude, deprivation of the familiar, or the clash of the new. In T. S. Eliot's words, "Old men should be explorers." It is not necessarily a young person's game. It may mean going abroad or into the Peace Corps, for example, or starting a new business. There are, after all, legions of managers over fifty recently released from their corporations and looking for new worlds. The ever-hopeful explorer is an innovator who does not easily give in to despair and self-pity.

The role of the minstrel is expressive, his mode joyous, emotive, dancelike. He understands underlying patterns, the melody of a process, and can "sing" that pattern for others. The minstrel role combines leadership with the narrative of song. He must be able to organize and structure information, and then communicate it. Such a role builds consensus. The minstrel is soothing, enchanting.

The jester uses wit, usually with a bite, to convey some underlying wisdom. A jester might be a holy kidder, whose links to a larger value or purpose makes her see the ironic humor in the world. Or she might serve as a mirror that allows people to see their own reflections in her wit. Jesters may speak in riddles like Zen koans, which present problems that cannot be resolved within the constraints of logic (for example, What did your face look like before your ancestors were born?). The jester offers comic relief from the burdens of the present, but with a moral bite between the laughs.

There is the intermediary role of priests or shamans, who have some unique, often mysterious access to regions beyond the routines of daily life that are important to the people they serve. Working within a hierarchy, the priest acts as transmitter of traditions, guarding the core of specialized knowledge. Rational, compassionate, understanding, he does not disturb the web of structure, but rather interprets it for others as well as serving as a gatekeeper to the numinous, the realm beyond normal experience. He is spiritual, but only within the constraints of a given order.

Unlike the priest, the shaman is intuitive and nonrational and seeks breakthroughs outside the established order. If a shaman is a balloon, a priest is a tether: each needs the other to be effective. The shaman is a prophet, thinking about the challenges of the future; she is a mysterious interpreter of the unseen for those who are stuck in the mundane world. Shamans are often not pleasant to be around because they do not fit accepted patterns. They have seen a vision beyond the moment and are on a mission.

The role of the healer is the most intensely consensus-building of all. The healer brings a special expertise, diagnostic skill, and deep understanding to problems. As a surgeon, an herbalist, a psychotherapist, she is a troubleshooter. In the business context, the healer might be the person everyone calls on to solve crises.

All these roles are metaphors straining to be myths. They offer guidelines to help us form our mode of being and acting in the world. They expand our personal boundaries, "upsize" us for the tasks at hand.

As significant change sweeps over every part of the world, global culture—or more precisely, a complex, interpenetrating set of global cultures—is swirling into constantly shifting shapes. Failure to create our own socially constructed reality to make sense of the world around us will result in personal stagnation, loss of position, and rigidity. We need new myths in order to succeed.

Electronic media have become a central force in our lives. Watching and understanding the world through television, we have come to internalize the grammar and meaning of the televised image, its fast editing, its persistence of vision, its saturated color. As we learned from the episodes of terrorism in the eighties, many world events are largely created by the presence of this medium through which our myths are communicated.

We cannot escape this fact. Screens of various sorts are a pervasive part of our global landscape, and the dramatic happenings of the last decade—the collapse of the Berlin Wall, the protests in Tienanmen Square, the Gulf War—would not have occurred without them. Social reality is made up of the global hallucination of our media, but it is a reality we all share. It has been said that perception is reality. As such, our actions through the mutually empowering media of computer networks, video telephone service, and facsimile transmission have an effect on the physical world.

Television simulates physical action; the fax machine simulates the original document (which, with computer-generated fax, doesn't really exist at all); a spreadsheet simulates the "what if" business process. We must gain an awareness that all these simulations are metaphors, the precursors of myth. One thing is equated with another, but their identities remain separate.

A simulation begins as a training exercise. It refers to something real—a skill, a process, a social or political action. The goal of many simulations is to approach as thoroughly as possible the real experience of the activity being simulated. The theorist Jean Baudrillard has suggested that electronic media, by fostering a world of simulation, have broken down the boundaries between simulation and reality. The simulation has taken over, become what he calls the "hyperreal." Now the simulation refers only to itself, not to anything in the real world. This is the dark side of virtual reality that attempts to offer the complete experience of reality itself, mediated through the computer, but with the computer refined out of awareness.[5]

Knowing this helps us act in the world. We can make a difference, in our own lives and in the lives of our fellow men and women, wherever they are.

Adaptable individuals will find new niches, create new opportunities derived from fresh and flexible views of reality. Their new hero roles will undoubtedly change, grow, and evolve over time. They may shift slightly in emphasis or style from one context to another. In the postmodern world, changing structures form an impermanent foundation. There are no absolutes in our cultural milieu: no God, state, or corporation is going to be handing them out. But new myths will grow, fueled by new genres of organizations, new genres of business heroes.

At the end of the annual clairvoyants' convention in Paris in 1978 a reporter asked one of the participants if there would be another meeting the following year. The clairvoyant replied, "We don't know yet."[6]

In such a world, the possibilities are provocative. Nobody can predict the future, but we can do a lot better than nothing. We are on our way to a slippery future in which many things will be possible. That is what the new anytime/anyplace, technological, electronic, mediated, interlinked, flexible and shifting, multicultural and diverse, boundaryless, puzzling, challenging, and uncertain world is all about. We need to step up to new roles, create new myths for ourselves, for our teams, and for our organizations. Job titles are obsolete, but new organizational roles are abundant.

Scientists who work on chaos theory and the mathematical analysis of complexity have noted that the stable region in the center of systems is dead; nothing new can emerge there. Outside the stable center, random and chaotic events rule. But at the edge, on the frontier between the stable center and the chaotic outside, new and exciting things happen. Innovation and growth is at the edges. In our interviews with people whose companies had been reengineered, we noticed over and over that the most productive and fulfilled people were those working at the edges of organizations. It is a dangerous time to be too close to the corporate center.

Those at the edges have taken responsibility for their lives. They are the upsized individuals. The future is theirs.

Notes

INTRODUCTION

1. Stanley M. Davis, *Future Perfect* (Reading, Mass.: Addison-Wesley, 1989).

CHAPTER 1

1. Robert B. Reich, quoted in Paul Leinberger and Bruce Tucker, *The New Individualists* (New York: HarperCollins, 1991), p. 210.

2. Ibid., p. 233.

3. Leinberger and Tucker, *The New Individualists*. For a description of how societies, like individuals, construct themselves see also Walter Truett Anderson, *Reality Isn't What It Used to Be: Theatrical Politics, Ready-to-Wear Religion, Global Myths, Primitive Chic, and Other Wonders of the Postmodern World* (New York: Harper & Row, 1990).

CHAPTER 2

1. Michael Hammer, "Reengineering Work: Don't Automate, Obliterate," *Harvard Business Review,* July/August 1990.

2. Michael Hammer and James Champy, *Reengineering the Corporation: A Manifesto for Business Revolution* (New York: HarperBusiness, 1993).

3. Gene Hall, Jim Rosenthal, and Judy Wade, "How to Make Reengineering Really Work," *Harvard Business Review,* November/December 1993, p. 119.

4. Peter G. W. Keen and Ellen M. Knapp, *Every Manager's Guide to Business Process Investment: A Glossary of Key Terms & Concepts for Today's Business Leader* (Boston: Harvard Business School Press, 1995).

5. Joseph Campbell, *The Hero with a Thousand Faces* (Princeton: Princeton University Press, 1949), p. 236.

6. Michael Rothschild, *Bionomics: The Inevitability of Capitalism* (New York: Holt, 1990). Rothschild's research led him to establish a consulting firm, the Bionomics Institute, in San Rafael, California.

7. Davis, *Future Perfect;* Stanley M. Davis and Bill Davidson, *2020 Vision* (New York: Simon & Schuster, 1991).

8. Davis, *Future Perfect*, pp. 5–6.

9. Peter G. W. Keen, "Telecommunications and Organizational Advantage," *Proceedings of the Harvard Colloquium on Global Competition and Telecommunications* (Cambridge: Harvard Business School, 1991).

10. *Fortune,* August 23, 1993, p. 52.

CHAPTER 3

1. See Richard L. Nolan, Alex J. Pollock, and James P. Ware, "Creating the Twenty-first Century Organization," *Stage by Stage* 8 (1988).

2. Raymond E. Miles and Charles C. Snow, "Organizations: New Concepts for New Forms," *California Management Review* 28 (Spring 1986).

3. *Harvard Business Review,* March/April 1991, p. 95.

4. Kenichi Ohmae, *The Borderless World: Power and Strategy in the Interlinked Economy* (New York: HarperBusiness, 1990).

5. Davis, *Future Perfect,* pp. 138–190.

6. "Some Leaders in Market Value Do a Disappearing Act," *Fortune,* May 3, 1993, p. 35.

CHAPTER 4

1. Davis, *Future Perfect,* pp. 10–89.

2. Quoted in Jack M. Nilles, "How to Plan For and Supervise Telecommuters," *Western City* (League of California Cities), February 1991, p. 4.

3. Nilles's work is summarized in his new book called *Making Telecommuting Happen* (New York: Van Nostrand Reinhold, 1994).

4. These forecasts, along with graphs charting the different scenarios, are available from Telecommuting Research Institute, Inc., 971 Stonehill Lane, Los Angeles, California 90049.

5. Quoted in Nilles, "How to Plan For and Supervise Telecommuters," p. 21.

6. State of California, Department of General Services, "The California Telecommuting Pilot Project Final Report," 1990, available from JALA Associates, Inc., 971 Stonehill Lane, Los Angeles, California 90049-1412.

CHAPTER 5

1. Cited in a talk by Andrew Hacker, professor of political science at Queens College, City University of New York, as part of the Chautauqua lecture series "Racism in America" on radio station KALW, January 25, 1994.

CHAPTER 6

1. Peter Senge, *The Fifth Discipline: The Art and Practice of the Learning Organization* (New York: Doubleday, 1990).

2. See, for example, W. Edwards Deming, *Out of the Crisis* (Cambridge: MIT Press, 1982); Philip B. Crosby, *Quality Is Free* (New York: Mentor, 1979). See also Joe Cullen and Jack Hollingum, *Implementing Total Quality* (Bedford, England: IFS Publications, 1987).

CHAPTER 7

1. William Bridges, *Surviving Corporate Transition* (Mill Valley, Calif.: Bridges & Associates, 1988).

CHAPTER 8

1. Carla O'Dell, "Team Play, Team Pay—New Ways of Keeping Score," *Across the Board*, November 1989, p. 38.

2. U.S. Department of Labor, Bureau of Labor Statistics, *Employee Benefits in Medium and Large Firms*, vols. for 1984–86 (Washington, D.C.: Government Printing Office, 1984–86). See also "Offering Employees Stock Options They Can't Refuse: More and More Companies Want Workers to Think Like Owners," *Business Week*, October 7, 1991.

CHAPTER 9

1. The research was part of a pioneering effort over a number of years by a group called the Communications Studies Group, led by Marton Elton at University College, London. The results are summarized in John A. Short, Ederyn Williams, and Bruce Christie, *The Social Psychology of Telecommunications* (London: Wiley & Sons, 1976).

CHAPTER 10

1. Larry Hirschhorn and Thomas Gilmore, "The New Boundaries of the 'Boundaryless' Company," *Harvard Business Review*, May/June 1992, p. 104.

2. John Markoff, "Invasion of Computer: 'Back Door' Left Ajar," *New York Times*, November 7, 1988.

3. Kapor and Barlow have founded a consumer interest group, the Electronic Frontiers Foundation, to protect the rights of consumers using the electronic information system. For more information write Electronic Frontiers Foundation, 356 West Twenty-third Street, New York, New York 10011 (e-mail: barlow@eff.org or barlow1@AOL.com).

CHAPTER 11

1. Quoted in "Odd Man Out" by Alan Deutschman, *Fortune*, July 26, 1993, p. 42.

2. Max DePree, *Leadership Is an Art* (New York: Dell, 1989), p. 111.

3. This conclusion is supported by Howard Rheingold, *The Virtual Community* (Reading, Mass.: Addison-Wesley, 1993). We have often witnessed the development of such romances via computer network over the past twenty years.

CHAPTER 12

1. U.S. Department of Commerce, Bureau of the Census, *Poverty in the United States* (Washington, D.C.: Government Printing Office, 1992), Table D-2.

2. U.S. Department of Commerce, Bureau of the Census, *Workers with Low Earnings* (Washington, D.C.: Government Printing Office, 1992).

3. *Computer Competence: The National Assessment*, National Assessment of Educational Programs, 1987.

4. U.S. Department of Commerce, Bureau of the Census, *Computer Use in the United States*, Current Population Reports, P-23 (Washington, D.C.: Government Printing Office, 1989).

5. U.S. Census Bureau, *Poverty in the United States*, Table 3.

6. Quoted in "Company School: As Pool of Skilled Help Tightens, Firms Move to Broaden Their Role," *Wall Street Journal*, May 8, 1989.

7. Douglas Coupland, *Generation X* (New York: St. Martin's, 1991).

CHAPTER 14

1. R. D. Cormia, "Information Technology, Storage and Processing, Past, Present and Future," paper presented at a seminar at Surface Science Laboratories, Moutain View, Calif., July 16, 1993.

2. Chris Argyris, "Teaching Smart People How to Learn," *Harvard Business Review*, May/June 1991, pp. 102–103.

CHAPTER 15

1. J. T. Fraser, *Time, the Familiar Stranger* (Redmond, Wash.: Tempus Books, 1987).

2. Ibid., p. xvi.

3. George Leonard, *Mastery: The Keys to Success and Long-Term Fulfillment* (New York: Plume, 1992), p. 33.

4. Fraser, *Time, the Familiar Stranger*, p. 313.

5. Ibid., p. 325.

CHAPTER 16

1. Quoted in Doug Bartholomew, "Charles Schwab: Bullish on Reengineering," *Information Week*, July 22, 1991, p. 12.

2. Eric K. Clemons and Michael C. Row, "Ahead of the Pack Through Vision and Hustle: A Case Study of Information Technology at Rosenbluth Travel," *Proceedings of the Twenty-fourth Annual Hawaii International Confer-*

ence on Systems Sciences (Los Alamitos, Calif.: IEEE Computer Society Press, 1971).

3. Quote in Ibid., p. 292.

4. Davis and Davidson, *2020 Vision.*

5. Quoted in Clemons and Row, "Ahead of the Pack," p. 291.

6. Quoted in Ibid., p. 293.

7. William H. Davidow and Michael S. Malone, *The Virtual Corporation: Structuring and Revitalizing the Corporation for the Twenty-first Century* (New York: HarperBusiness, 1992).

8. William Poundstone, *Prisoner's Dilemma: John von Neumann, Game Theory, and the Puzzle of the Bomb* (New York: Doubleday, 1992), p. 6.

9. See, for example, Richard Beckhard and Wendy Pritchard, *Changing the Essence: The Art of Creating and Leading Fundamental Change in Organizations* (San Francisco: Jossey-Bass, 1992), which nicely summarizes Beckhard's ideas regarding organizational change.

10. Ohmae, *The Borderless World*, p. 90.

11. Ibid., p. 72.

CHAPTER 18

1. Lynda M. Applegate, James I. Cash, Jr., and D. Quinn Mills, "Information Technology and Tomorrow's Manager," *Harvard Business Review*, November/December 1988, pp. 128–136.

2. Anderson, *Reality Isn't What It Used to Be.*

3. The Bellcore research has pursued a "video window" strategy. The work at the University of Arizona is part of the Mirror Project in the Department of Management Information Systems, College of Business and Public Administration. Keio University in Yokohama, Japan, is also attempting to create social presence at a distance with its MAJIC system, which is being developed by Yutaka Matsushita.

4. A. Michael Noll, "Teleportation Through Communications," *Correspondence of the Institute of Electrical and Electronics Engineers*, Annals 611SM006, 1976.

5. Brenda Laurel, "The Role of Drama in the Evolution of Virtual Reality," speech presented at the first annual Virtual Reality Conference, San Francisco, December 1990.

6. Quoted in Steven Levy, "Brave New World: Man, Machine, and Music," *Rolling Stone*, June 14, 1990.

7. Brenda Laurel, *Computers as Theater* (Reading, Mass.: Addison-Wesley, 1991).

8. Max Hopper gained his fame at American Airlines, where he is credited with the dramatic success and competitive advantages of the SABRE computerized airline reservation system. See "Rattling SABRE—New Ways to Compete on Information," *Harvard Business Review,* May–June 1990.

9. Michihiro Matsumoto, *The Unspoken Way* (Tokyo and New York: Kodansha International, 1988), 27. As Americans, we have found Matsumoto's book an extremely useful introduction to the concept of *haragei.*

CHAPTER 19

1. Edward T. Hall, *The Silent Language* (Garden City, N.Y.: Anchor Books Ed: 1973), p. xviii.

2. Robert Levering and Milton Moskowitz, *The 100 Best Companies to Work for in America* (New York: Currency Doubleday, 1993), p. 107.

3. Ohmae, *The Borderless World,* p. 99.

4. Rosabeth Moss Kanter, "The New Managerial Work," *Harvard Business Review,* November/December 1989.

5. Quoted in "GE Keeps Those Ideas Coming," by Thomas A. Stewart, *Fortune,* August 12, 1991, p. 49.

6. Joan A. Rigdon, "Managing," *Wall Street Journal,* August 18, 1993.

7. National Opinion Research Center, General Social Survey, University of Connecticut, August, 1993.

8. Ellen Galinsky, James T. Bond, and Dana E. Friedman, *The Changing Workforce* (New York: Families and Work Institute, 1993), p. 16.

9. Quoted in Lynda M. Applegate and James I. Cash, "GE Canada: Designing a New Organization," Harvard Business School Case 9-189-138, 1989, p. 1.

10. "AT&T Capital: Life on the Leading Edge," *Perspectives* 3 (1991), pp. 12–13.

CHAPTER 20

1. Richard G. O'Lone, "777 Revolutionizes Boeing Aircraft Development Process," *Aviation Week and Space Technology,* June 3, 1991, p. 34.

2. C. K. Prahalad and Gary Hamel, "The Core Competence of the Corporation," *Harvard Business Review,* May/June 1990, p. 82.

3. Mark S. Ackerman and Thomas W. Malone, "Answer Garden: A Tool for Growing Organizational Memory," paper presented at the ACM Conference on Office Information Systems, Cambridge, Mass., April 1990.

4. James M. Laffey, N. Rao Machiraju, and Ravinder Chandhok, "Organizational Memory as a Support Tool for Learning and Performance: Prototypes and Issues," *Proceedings of the International Conference on Learning Sciences,* Evanston, Ill.: Association for the Advancement of Computing in Education, August 4–7, 1991.

5. This research is being conducted at the Centre for Applied Cognitive Science, Ontario Institute for Studies in Education, Toronto. A good overview of the research and early results is contained in Marlene Scardamalia and Carl Bereiter, "Higher Levels of Agency for Children in Knowledge Building: A Challenge for the Deisgn of New Knowledge Media," *Journal of Learning Sciences,* Volume 1, No. 1, 1991.

CHAPTER 21

1. Brian Arthur, "Positive Feedbacks in the Economy," *Scientific American,* February 1990, p. 92.

2. Interview with Bill Walsh, Menlo Park, California, October 15, 1991. Walsh's approach to management is summarized in his book *Building a Champion* (New York: St. Martin's, 1990).

3. Jeremy Rifkin, *Time Wars* (New York: Holt, 1987), chap. 1.

CHAPTER 22

1. Quoted in "The Logic of Global Business: An Interview with ABB's Percy Barnevik," by William Taylor, *Harvard Business Review,* March–April 1991, p. 96.

CHAPTER 23

1. Mary O'Hara-Devereaux's extensive research on cross-cultural work teams in global organizations is well documented in the book she co-authored with Robert Johansen, *GlobalWork* (San Francisco: Jossey-Bass, 1994), which gives guidelines for how to establish common frames of reference among diverse workers.

CHAPTER 24

1. Eric K. Clemons, "Information Technology and the Boundary of the Firm: Who Wins, Who Loses, Who Has to Change," *Proceedings of the Harvard Colloquium on Global Competition and Telecommunications* (Cambridge: Harvard Business School, 1991). p. 17.

2. Mark Stefik and John Seely Brown, "Toward Portable Ideas," in *Technological Support for Work Group Collaboration,* ed. Margrethe H. Olson (Hillsdale, N.J.: Erlbaum Associates, 1989).

CHAPTER 25

1. Mircea Eliade, *Myths, Dreams, and Mysteries* (New York: Harper & Row, 1960), p. 15.

2. Bill Moyers, foreword to Joseph Campbell with Bill Moyers, *The Power of Myth* (New York: Doubleday, 1988), p. xvi.

3. Robert B. Reich, "Entrepreneurship Reconsidered: The Team as Hero," *Harvard Business Review,* May/June 1987.

4. Erving Goffman, *The Presentation of Self in Everyday Life* (New York: Doubleday Anchor, 1959).

5. Jean Baudrillard, "Simulacra and Simulations," in *Selected Writings,* ed. Mark Poster (Stanford: Stanford University Press, 1988).

6. Stephen Pile, *The Incomplete Book of Failures* (New York: Dutton, 1979), p. 44.

Bibliography

Ackerman, Mark S., and Thomas W. Malone. "Answer Garden: A Tool for Growing Organizational Memory." Paper presented at the ACM Conference on Office Information Systems, Cambridge, Mass., April 1990.

Anderson, Walter Truett. *Reality Isn't What It Used to Be: Theatrical Politics, Ready-to-Wear Religion, Global Myths, Primitive Chic, and Other Wonders of the Postmodern World*. New York: Harper & Row, 1990.

Applegate, Lynda M., James I. Cash, Jr., and D. Quinn Mills. "Information Technology and Tomorrow's Manager." *Harvard Business Review*, November/December 1988.

Applegate, Lynda M., and James I. Cash. "GE Canada: Designing a New Organization." Harvard Business School Case 9-189-138, 1989.

Argyris, Chris. "Teaching Smart People How to Learn." *Harvard Business Review*, May/June 1991.

Arthur, Brian. "Positive Feedbacks in the Economy." *Scientific American*, February 1990.

"AT&T Capital: Life on the Leading Edge." *Perspectives* 3 (1991).

Bartholomew, Doug. "Charles Schwab: Bullish on Reengineering." *Information Week*, July 22, 1991.

Baudrillard, Jean. "Simulacra and Simulations." *Selected Writings*. Edited by Mark Poster. Stanford: Stanford University Press, 1988.

Beckhard, Richard, and Wendy Pritchard. *Changing the Essence: The Art of Creating and Leading Fundamental Change in Organizations*. San Francisco: Jossey-Bass, 1992.

Bridges, William. *Surviving Corporate Transition*. Mill Valley, Calif.: Bridges & Associates, 1988.

Bullen, Christine V., and John F. Rockart. "A Primer on Critical Success Factors." Center for Information Systems Research Working Paper no. 69, Sloan School of Management, MIT, June 1981.

Burgelman, Robert A., and Leonard R. Sayles. *Inside Corporate Innovation: Strategies, Structure, and Managerial Skills*. New York: Free Press, 1986.

California, State of. Department of General Services. "The California Telecommuting Pilot Project Final Report." JALA Associates, Los Angeles, 1990.

Campbell, Joseph. *The Hero with a Thousand Faces*. Princeton: Princeton University Press, 1949.

Campbell, Joseph, with Bill Moyers. *The Power of Myth*. New York: Doubleday, 1988.

Cash, James I., and Poppy L. McLeod. "Managing the Introduction of Information Systems Technology in Strategically Dependent Companies." *Journal of Management Information Systems* 1 (Spring 1985).

Cash, James I., Robert G. Eccles, Nitin Nohira, and Richard L. Nolan. *Building the Information-Age Organization: Structure, Control, and Information Technologies*. Boston: Harvard Business School Press, 1994.

Christensen, Kathleen. "A Hard Day's Work in the Electronic Cottage." *Across the Board*, April 1987.

Clemons, Eric K. "Information Technology and the Boundary of the Firm: Who Wins, Who Loses, Who Has to Change." *Proceedings of the Harvard Colloquium on Global Competition and Telecommunications*. Cambridge: Harvard Business School, 1991.

Clemons, Eric K., and Michael C. Row. "Ahead of the Pack Through Vision and Hustle: A Case Study of Information Technology at Rosenbluth Travel." *Proceedings of the Twenty-Fourth Annual Hawaii International Conference on Systems Sciences*. vol. 4. Los Alamitos, Calif.: IEEE Computer Society Press, 1971.

"Company School: As Pool of Skilled Help Tightens, Firms Move to Broaden Their Role." *Wall Street Journal*, May 8, 1989.

Copeland, Lennie, and Lewis Griggs. *Going International: How to Make Friends and Deal Effectively in the Global Marketplace*. New York: Random House, 1985.

Cormia, R. D. "Information Technology, Storage and Processing, Past, Present and Future." Paper presented at a seminar at Surface Science Laboratories, Mountain View, Calif., July 1993.

Coupland, Douglas. *Generation X*. New York: St. Martin's, 1991.

Crosby, Philip B. *Quality Is Free*. New York: Mentor, 1979.

Cullen, Joe, and Jack Hollingum. *Implementing Total Quality*. Bedford, England: IFS Publications, 1987.

Davidow, William H., and Michael S. Malone. *The Virtual Corporation: Structuring and Revitalizing the Corporation for the Twenty-first Century*. New York: HarperBusiness, 1992.

Davis, Stanley M. *Future Perfect*. Reading, Mass.: Addison-Wesley, 1987.

Davis, Stanley M., and Bill Davidson. *2020 Vision*. New York: Simon & Schuster, 1991.

DeMarco, Tom, and Timothy Lister. *Peopleware: Productive Projects and Teams.* New York: Dorset, 1987.

Deming, W. Edwards. *Out of the Crisis.* Cambridge: MIT Press, 1982.

DePree, Max. *Leadership Is an Art.* New York: Dell, 1989.

Drexler, Allan B., David Sibbet, and Russell H. Forrester. "The Team Performance Model." In *Team Building: Blueprints for Productivity and Satisfaction.* Edited by W. Brendan Reddy. Alexandria, Va.: National Institute for Applied Behavioral Science, 1988.

Drucker, Peter F. "The Coming of the New Organization." *Harvard Business Review,* January/February 1988.

———. *The New Realities.* New York: Harper & Row, 1989.

Dyer, William G. *Team Building: Issues and Alternatives.* Reading, Mass.: Addison-Wesley, 1987.

Eliade, Mircea. *Myths, Dreams, and Mysteries.* New York: Harper & Row, 1960.

Engelbart, Douglas C. "A Conceptual Framework for the Augmentation of Man's Intellect." In *Vistas in Information Handling,* vol. 1. Edited by Paul W. Howerton. Washington, D.C.: Spartan Books, 1963.

Fisher, Scott S. "Virtual Interface Environments." In *The Art of Human-Computer Interface Design.* Edited by Brenda Laurel. Reading, Mass.: Addison-Wesley, 1990.

Fraser, J. T. *Time, the Familiar Stranger.* Redmond, Wash.: Tempus Books, 1987.

Galinsky, Ellen, James T. Bond, and Dana E. Friedman. *The Changing Workforce.* New York: Families and Work Institute, 1993.

Goffman, Erving. *The Presentation of Self in Everyday Life.* New York: Doubleday Anchor, 1959.

Goodman, Paul S., Lee S. Sproull, et al. *Technology and Organizations.* San Francisco: Jossey-Bass, 1990.

Grenier, Ray, and George Metes. *Enterprise Networking: Working Together Apart.* Bedford, Mass.: Digital Press, 1992.

Hall, Edward T. *The Silent Language.* Garden City, N.Y.: Doubleday, 1959.

Hall, Gene, Jim Rosenthal, and Judy Wade. "How to Make Reengineering Really Work." *Harvard Business Review,* November/December 1993.

Hammer, Michael. "Reengineering Work: Don't Automate, Obliterate." *Harvard Business Review,* July/August 1990.

Hammer, Michael, and James Champy. *Reengineering the Corporation: A Manifesto for Business Revolution.* New York: HarperBusiness, 1993.

Hampden-Turner, Charles. *Charting the Corporate Mind: Graphic Solutions to Business Conflicts.* New York: Free Press, 1990.

Hanna, David P. *Designing Organizations for High Performance.* Reading, Mass.: Addison-Wesley, 1988.

Harman, Willis. *Global Mind Change: The New Age Revolution in the Way We Think.* New York: Warner, 1990.

Harvard Business Review, March/April 1991.

Helsel, Sandra K., and Judith Paris Roth, eds. *Virtual Reality: Theory, Practice, and Promise.* Westport, Conn.: Meckler, 1991.

Hirschhorn, Larry, and Thomas Gilmore. "The New Boundaries of the 'Boundaryless' Company." *Harvard Business Review,* May/June 1992.

Ives, Blake, and Sirkka L. Jarvenpaa. "Applications of Global Information Technology: Key Issues for Management." *MIS Quarterly,* March 1991.

Johansen, Robert, Jacques Vallee, and Kathleen Spangler. *Electronic Meetings.* Reading, Mass.: Addison-Wesley, 1979.

Johansen, Robert, David Sibbet, Suzyn Benson, Alexia Martin, Robert Mittman, and Paul Saffo. *Leading Business Teams.* Reading, Mass.: Addison-Wesley, 1991.

Johansen, Robert, and Mary O'Hara-Devereaux. *GlobalWork.* San Francisco: Jossey-Bass, 1994.

Kanter, Rosabeth Moss. *The Change Masters: Innovation and Entrepreneurship in the American Corporation.* New York: Simon & Schuster, 1983.

———."The New Managerial Work." *Harvard Business Review,* November/December 1989.

Kayser, Thomas A. *Mining Group Gold.* El Segundo, Calif.: Serif, 1990.

Keen, Peter G. W. "Telecommunications and Organizational Advantage." *Proceedings of the Harvard Colloquium on Global Competition and Telecommunications,* Los Alamitos, Calif.: IEEE Computer Society Press, 1971.

Keen, Peter G. W. and Ellen M. Knapp. *Business Process Investment: Getting the Right Process Right.* Boston: Harvard Business School Press, 1995.

Kotkin, Joel. *Tribes: How Race, Religion and Identity Determine Success in the New Global Economy.* New York: Random House, 1992.

Kraut, Robert E. "Telecommuting: The Tradeoff of Home Work." *Journal of Communications* 39 (Summer 1989).

———, ed. *Technology and the Transformation of White-Collar Work.* Hillsdale, N.J.: Erlbaum Associates, 1987.

Laffey, James M., N. Rao Machiraju, and Ravinder Chandhok. "Organizational Memory as a Support Tool for Learning and Performance: Prototypes and Issues." *Proceedings of the International Conference on Learning Sciences.* Evanston, Illinois: Association for the Advancement of Computing in Education, August 4–7, 1991.

Larson, Carl E., and Frank M. J. LaFasto. *TeamWork: What Must Go Right/What Can Go Wrong.* Newbury Park, Calif.: Sage, 1989.

Leinberger, Paul, and Bruce Tucker. *The New Individualists.* New York: Harper-Collins, 1991.

Leonard, George. *Mastery: The Keys to Success and Long-Term Fulfillment.* New York: Plume, 1992.

Levering, Robert, and Milton Moskowitz. *The 100 Best Companies to Work for in America.* New York: Currency Doubleday, 1993.

Levy, Steven. "Brave New World: Man, Machine, and Music." *Rolling Stone,* June 14, 1990.

McFarlan, F. W., and J. L. McKenney. "The Information Archipelago—Maps and Bridges." *Harvard Business Review,* September/October 1982.

McLuhan, Marshall, and Quentin Fiore. *War and Peace in the Global Village.* New York: Bantam, 1968.

Malone, Thomas W. "What Is Coordination Theory?" Center for Information Systems Research Working Paper no. 182, Sloan School of Management, MIT, February 1988.

Markoff, John. "Invasion of Computer: 'Back Door' Left Ajar." *New York Times,* November 7, 1988.

Matsumoto, Michihiro. *The Unspoken Way.* Tokyo and New York: Kodansha International, 1988.

Morrison, Philip, Kosta Tsipis, and Jerome Wiesner. "The Future of American Defense." *Scientific American,* February 1994.

Miles, Raymond E., and Charles C. Snow. "Organizations: New Concepts for New Forms." *California Management Review* 28, (Spring 1986).

Nilles, Jack M. "How to Plan for and Supervise Telecommuters." *Western City* (League of California Cities), February 1991.

———. *Making Telecommuting Happen.* New York: Von Nostrand Reinhold, 1994.

Nolan, R. L., and C. F. Gibson. "Managing the Four Stages of EDP Growth." *Harvard Business Review,* March/April, 1979.

Nolan, Richard L., Alex J. Pollock, and James P. Ware. "Creating the Twenty-first Century Organization." *Stage by Stage* 8 (1988).

Noll, A. Michael. "Teleportation Through Communications." *Correspondence of the Institute of Electrical and Electronics Engineers.* Annals 611SM006, 1976.

O'Dell, Carla. "Team Play, Team Pay—New Ways of Keeping Score," *Across the Board,* November, 1989.

"Offering Employees Stock Options They Can't Refuse: More and More Companies Want Workers to Think Like Owners." *Business Week,* October 7, 1991.

Ohmae, Kenichi. *The Borderless World: Power and Strategy in the Interlinked Economy.* New York: HarperBusiness, 1990.

O'Lone, Richard G. "777 Revolutionizes Boeing Aircraft Development Process." *Aviation Week and Space Technology,* June 3, 1991.

Palvia, Shailendra, Prashant Palvia, and Ronald M. Zigli, eds. *The Global Issues of Information Technology Management.* Harrisburg, Penn.: Idea Group Publishing, 1992.

Pascal, Richard Tanner. *Managing on the Edge: How the Smartest Companies Use Conflict to Stay Ahead.* New York: Simon & Schuster, 1990.

Pile, Stephen. *The Incomplete Book of Failures.* New York: Dutton, 1979.

Piore, Michael J., and Charles F. Sabel. *The Second Industrial Divide: Possibilities for Prosperity.* New York: Basic Books, 1984.

Poundstone, William. *Prisoner's Dilemma: John von Neumann, Game Theory, and the Puzzle of the Bomb.* New York: Doubleday, 1992.

Prahalad, C. K., and Gary Hamel. "The Core Competence of the Corporation." *Harvard Business Review,* May/June 1990.

Preminger, Alex. *The Princeton Encyclopedia of Poetry and Poetics.* Princeton, N.J.: Princeton University Press, 1974.

"Rattling SABRE—New Ways to Compete on Information." *Harvard Business Review,* May/June 1990.

Reich, Robert B. *The Next American Frontier.* New York: Times Books, 1983.

———. "Entrepreneurship Reconsidered: The Team As Hero." *Harvard Business Review,* May/June 1987.

Rheingold, Howard. *The Virtual Community.* Reading, Mass.: Addison-Wesley, 1993.

———. *Virtual Reality.* New York: Summit Books, 1991.

Richman, Tom. "Mrs. Fields' Secret Ingredient." *Inc. Magazine,* October 1987.

Rifkin, Jeremy. *Time Wars.* New York: Holt, 1987.

Rigdon, Joan A. "Managing." *Wall Street Journal,* August 18, 1993.

Rothschild, Michael. *Bionomics: The Inevitability of Capitalism.* New York: Holt, 1990.

Scardamalia, Marlene, and Carl Bereiter. "Higher Levels of Agency for Children in Knowledge Building: A Challenge for the Design of New Knowledge Media." *Journal of Learning Sciences 1,* (1), 1991.

Schaef, Anne Wilson, and Diane Fassel. *The Addictive Organization*. San Francisco: Harper & Row, 1988.

Schwartz, Felice N. " 'Mommy Track': Management Women and the New Facts of Life." *Harvard Business Review*, January/February 1989.

Scott Morton, Michael S., ed. *The Corporation of the 1990s: Information Technology and Organizational Transformation*. New York: Oxford University Press, 1991.

Selz, Michael. "Small Companies Thrive by Taking Over Some Specialized Tasks for Big Concerns." *Wall Street Journal*, September 11, 1991.

Senge, Peter. *The Fifth Discipline: The Art and Practice of the Learning Organization*. New York: Doubleday, 1990.

Short, John A., Ederyn Williams, and Bruce Christie. *The Social Psychology of Telecommunications*. London: Wiley & Sons, 1976.

"Some Leaders in Market Do a Disappearing Act." *Fortune*, May 3, 1993.

Stefik, Mark, and John Seely Brown. "Toward Portable Ideas." In *Technological Support for Work Group Collaboration*. Edited by Margrethe H. Olson. Hillsdale, N.J.: Erlbaum Associates, 1989.

Stewart, Thomas A. "GE Keeps Those Ideas Coming," *Fortune*, August 12, 1991.

Streeter, Lynn A., and Karen E. Lochbaum. "An Expert/Expert-Locating System Based on Automatic Representation of Semantic Structure." *Proceedings of the Fourth Conference on Artificial Intelligence Applications*. Washington, D.C.: IEEE Computer Society, 1988.

Thorngren, Bertil. "Silent Actors—Communications Networks for Development." In *Social Impact of the Telephone*. Edited by Ithiel de Sola Pool. Cambridge, Mass.: MIT Press, 1977.

Toffler, Alvin. *Future Shock*. New York: Random House, 1970.

Traub, Joseph, ed. *Cohabiting with Computers*. Los Altos, Calif.: William Kaufmann, 1985.

Travers, P. L. *The World of the Hero*. Mount Kisko, N.Y.: Tamarack, 1993.

Turney, Peter B. B., and Bruce Anderson. "Accounting for Continuous Improvement." *Sloan Management Review*, Winter 1989.

U.S. Department of Commerce. Bureau of the Census. *Poverty in the United States*. Washington, D.C.: Government Printing Office, 1992.

———. *Workers with Low Earnings*. Washington, D.C.: Government Printing Office, 1992.

U.S. Department of Education. Office of Educational Research and Improvement. Office of Educational Research and Improvement. National Center for Education Statistics. *Digest of Education Statistics*. Vols. for 1987, 1988. Washington, D.C.: Government Printing Office, 1987–88.

U.S. Department of Labor. Bureau of Labor Statistics. *Employee Benefits in Medium and Large Firms.* Vols. for 1984–86. Washington, D.C.: Government Printing Office, 1984–86.

Waldrop, M. Mitchell. *Complexity: The Emerging Science at the Edge of Order and Chaos.* New York: Simon & Schuster, 1992.

Walsh, Bill. *Building a Champion.* New York: St. Martin's, 1990.

Index